WHITE SOX
ESSENTIAL

WHITE SOX ESSENTIAL

Everything You Need to Know
to Be a Real Fan!

Lew Freedman

TRIUMPH
BOOKS

Library of Congress Cataloging-in-Publication Data

Freedman, Lew.
    White Sox essential : everything you need to know to be a real
    fan! / Lew Freedman.
        p. cm.
    ISBN-13: 978-1-57243-932-0
    ISBN-10: 1-57243-932-7
    1. Chicago White Sox (Baseball team)—Miscellanea. 2. Chicago
    White Sox (Baseball team)—History. I. Title.

GV875.C58F74 2007
796.357'640977311—dc22

                                                        2006034209

This book is available in quantity at special discounts for your group or organization. For further information, contact:

Triumph Books
542 South Dearborn Street
Suite 750
Chicago, Illinois 60605
(312) 939-3330
Fax (312) 663-3557

Printed in U.S.A.
ISBN: 978-1-57243-932-0
Design by Patricia Frey
All photos courtesy of AP/Wide World Photos except where otherwise indicated

For the millions of White Sox fans who waited 88 years from 1917 to 2005 to see their team win another World Series title. Bless them for their patience and commitment.

And for all of those White Sox fans who lived and died in between and never got the chance to see their favorites win it all.

Contents

Acknowledgments

Special thanks to Scott Reifert, White Sox vice president of communications, for providing access to games for research, and, as always, a big thank-you to the research gang at the Baseball Hall of Fame Library in Cooperstown, New York.

It was both enjoyable and fruitful to review more than 100 years of files about the White Sox, their owners, their players, and their playoffs dating back to 1900 when Charles Comiskey brought the club to Chicago from St. Paul, Minnesota.

It was both a pleasure and informational gold mine to discuss White Sox history with author-editor Bob Vanderberg, Chicago baseball radio guru Bruce Levine, Hall of Fame shortstop Luis Aparicio, and ex–Sox players who still cheer for their old team, like Billy Pierce, Bob Shaw, Jim Landis, Jim Rivera, Turk Lown, Gerry Staley, Scott Fletcher, Eric Soderholm, Joel Horlen, La Marr Hoyt, Chet Lemon, and Wilbur Wood.

All helped to recapture old times as they relived good times and big games. It would have been even more fun if Bill Veeck were still around. The two-time team owner was probably cheering louder than anybody from somewhere up above when the White Sox won the 2005 World Series.

Introduction

White pieces of confetti blew through the air like giant snowflakes, piling up on downtown streets in a blizzard that matched the deepest snowfall in Chicago history. The wait was over and the celebration was New Year's Eve multiplied by a factor of 10.

Citizens from all around Chicago massed along the parade route 2 million strong—nearly as many people as had watched the Chicago White Sox play 81 home games at U.S. Cellular Field all season long from April to October. Two million. They jammed the side streets and the main streets, State Street that great street, and especially Wacker and LaSalle, where the players, A.J. and Paulie, Jose C. and Juan Uribe, stood proudly, and (if they brought a telescope or binoculars) the devotees might glimpse Ozzie, or even hear a few of his joyful words to cap the magic season.

Fans of every age, from the octogenarians who never thought they would live to see the day to toddlers whose parents did not think they should miss this day, partied madly to celebrate the end of the drought. Since 1917's last grand World Series championship victory, it had been 88 years—more than twice as long as Moses wandered in the desert. True believers thought this occasion, too, might have benefited from divine intervention.

When the Chicago White Sox captured the 2005 World Series championship, it punctuated a lifelong pilgrimage for fans with long memories, strong hearts, infinite patience, and South Side commitment worthy of the reminder that *fan* is short for fanatic. They had suffered quietly as America embraced the cuddly Cubs, who had not tasted World Series champagne since 1908. They had suffered inwardly as America embraced the lovable Red Sox, who had not tasted World Series Dom Perignon since 1918. Once in a while, as a new generation of White Sox teased them with an American League pennant or division title, the cry of "What about us?" strangled aborning in their throats.

For decades, White Sox fans grimly paid their penance for the Black Sox Scandal of 1919, the betting conspiracy resulting in a thrown World Series and expulsion from the sport of several of the team's top players, including the great Shoeless Joe Jackson. With glee, the franchise introduced the Go-Go White Sox of Luis Aparicio and Nellie Fox to the nation in the 1950s, complete with campy theme song, only to lose the 1959 World Series to the Los Angeles Dodgers. It took 46 years for the team to earn a return Series engagement.

It was an endurance test of a journey, not only for fans, but also for White Sox stars, such as Luke Appling, Aparicio, Fox, and Billy Pierce, all denied the game's biggest prize in a Sox uniform. There were marvelous moments, but no season-ending, righteous finale where the White Sox were the last men standing. Worse, during those years, the crosstown Chicago Cubs became the country's darling, its old-style, frozen-in-time Wrigley Field home a symbol of baseball the way it was and the way many felt it should be. White Sox fans felt like second-class residents in their own town—and despised it.

Then, in October 2005, the present generation of White Sox, grittily adhering to a script written by manager Ozzie Guillen, bestowed the greatest gift of all on a worshipful baseball fan—the gleaming gold World Series trophy.

When the massive crowd flooded the rally site on October 28, just days after the Sox swept the Houston Astros, fans chanted "White Sox! White Sox!" They quieted long enough to digest the words of appreciation conveyed by Manager of the Year Guillen, the one-time star shortstop returned to revive his old team.

Showered with adulation, Guillen possessed a pure understanding of both the passion and patience of those assembled before him. He summed up the moment perfectly. "Thank you, guys, for waiting so long," he said. "Thank God we did it for you guys."

And 2 million roared, laughed, and cried. For the first time since 1917, the White Sox were the kings of baseball.

Beginnings

In the 21st century, the name Comiskey has disappeared from all things White Sox—except for the bronze statue honoring the team's founder that stands behind the center-field seats at U.S. Cellular Field. However, there would be no Chicago White Sox without Comiskey and the Comiskey family.

Charles A. Comiskey gave birth to the franchise that graces Chicago's South Side, even as his partner Ban Johnson acted as midwife in creation of the American League. The roots of the White Sox date to the turn of the last century, when Comiskey struck a deal to move his St. Paul, Minnesota, team to Chicago to begin play in 1900, though the AL was still a minor league that season.

Comiskey was forced into a hard bargain with James A. Hart, at the time owner of the team that came to be called the Chicago Cubs. In order to move his baseball team to the Windy City, Comiskey had to agree to forego use of "Chicago" and agree not to play in a ballpark that was situated north of 35th Street. The arrangement is the origin of the South Side White Sox and the North Side Cubs. And while no one envisioned suburban sprawl in 1900 or any temptation to build a ballpark far from downtown, the newest White Sox park, opened in 1991, is still located at 35th Street.

Since he couldn't publicly identify his team as "Chicago," Comiskey cleverly adopted a strategy to resonate with long-time baseball fans. His club's nickname became the White Stockings, once the name of the Chicago National League franchise. Soon the nickname was shortened to White Sox.

Comiskey was a baseball man in his soul. Born August 15, 1859, he became a major personality in the early days of major league

Charles Comiskey's Hall of Fame plaque at the National Baseball Hall of Fame in Cooperstown, New York.

baseball, graduating from player to manager to owner. By the time Comiskey turned 20 he had committed his life and career to baseball. He was initially a pitcher, went on to become an accomplished first baseman with the old St. Louis Browns, then managed the team, and was an early proponent of sliding into bases head first. Comiskey was also innovative fielding around the bag.

Charles Murphy, a later Cubs owner, admired Comiskey's skill, writing, "He was a truly wonderful first baseman and really revolutionized the playing at that position, showing creative genius." While managing the Cincinnati Reds, Murphy said Comiskey was hugely popular. "I guess Comiskey could have been elected mayor at that time if he had aspired to a political career."

A four-time American Association pennant-winning manager who couldn't sit still, Comiskey once was the victim of a player's practical joke. A nail was driven up from the bottom of the bench and as he slid back and forth, Comiskey ripped his trousers. He did not notice the injury to his suit until after the game.

Baseball coped with uncertainty from the 1880s until stability arrived with the formation of the American League as a major league in 1901. Teams went bankrupt and died. Leagues came and went. Player union attempts fizzled. Comiskey, however, played ball with the winners and survivors, and for him life did begin at 40.

Nicknamed "the Old Roman," Comiskey was an admired figure in Chicago and in baseball (until the Black Sox Scandal). His major league Chicago club made its debut on April 24, 1901, against the Cleveland Blues. The Sox won 8–2. It was the first game ever played in the major league American League because three other games were rained out. Some White Sox notables in the lineup were Dummy Hoy, Fielder Jones, and Clark Griffith, who was a player-manager. Griffith, a future Hall of Famer, jumped from the already-established National League and finished 24–7 in his first White Sox pitching campaign.

Compiling an 83–53 record, the White Sox won the first American League pennant in 1901, but there was no World Series yet.

One of the great early stars of the White Sox was a colorful fellow named Guy Harris "Doc" White. More than a century after his pitching career began with the Philadelphia Phillies in 1901 and his move to the Sox in 1903, Doc White's name remains plastered all over the White Sox team-leader pitching lists. During his 13 seasons in the majors, the southpaw won 189 games.

White attended Georgetown University and earned a dental degree—and his nickname. He practiced dentistry during the off-season during the first five years of his baseball career, but White possessed

TRIVIA

Who pitched the first three no-hitters in White Sox history by 1908?

Answers to the trivia questions are on page 173.

many talents besides throwing a good fastball and sinker and the ability to control both. One year White designed the White Sox uniforms. He collaborated with famed sportswriter Ring Lardner on songs, and White sang the tunes in vaudeville performances. Later in life, White, who lived to be nearly 90 years old, owned minor league teams in Texas and taught physical education and coached baseball and basketball at Wilson Teachers College in Washington, D.C.

TOP 10

White Sox Most Games Started

	Player	# of Games
1.	Ted Lyons	484
2.	Red Faber	483
3.	Billy Pierce	390
4.	Ed Walsh	312
5.	Doc White	301
6.	Wilbur Wood	286
7.	Joel Horlen	284
8.	Ed Cicotte	258
9.	Richard Dotson	250
10.	Thornton Lee	232

White won 27 games for the White Sox during the 1907 season and in 1904 pitched a major league record five shutouts in a row. The record stood for 64 years. In 1912 White told a newspaper reporter why he thought so many baseball people believe left-handed pitchers have the advantage over left-handed hitters—a theory still in vogue today.

"It's the simplest thing in the world," White said. "The majority of the pitchers in the big leagues are right-handed, are they not? When you were a kid and played lots, the majority of pitchers then were right-handed, were they not? Admitting that, isn't it reasonable to assume that a ballplayer from his earliest days to the time he gets into the big leagues hits against right-handed pitchers twice as often as southpaws? Well, that's the answer and that's all there is to it."

During his early days as an owner, Comiskey, who was called Charlie when he played and compiled a .264 lifetime average, was regarded as a bon vivant. Sportswriters enjoyed his company and he shared liquor in his office with them. Other owners and baseball men respected his business savvy. A. J. Reach, founder of a sporting goods company and co-owner of the Philadelphia Athletics with Connie Mack, praised Comiskey lavishly in the 1919 biography *Commy* written by journalist G. W. Axelson. Reach suggested Comiskey "stands out as a great national heroic figure."

4

Reach speculated that Comiskey was the "richest individual club owner in the country—all achieved by his own labor and effort in the face of many discouragements."

There was no doubt the White Sox were a personal fiefdom until Comiskey died in Eagle River, Wisconsin, in 1931. Heirs of the founder kept the team in the family for just shy of an additional three decades.

For all of his success as player and manager and his milestone accomplishment of imbedding the White Sox into Chicago's culture, Comiskey's reign by no means peaked with the 1901 pennant. On Commy's watch, the Sox pulled off one of the greatest World Series upsets of all time—with special thanks to a mound magician named Big Ed Walsh—and built one of the great monuments of sporting architecture. The grand baseball palace called Comiskey Park was modeled after the Roman Coliseum. Comiskey was indeed the emperor of a great empire.

By the NUMBERS **354,350**—During its first year of major league play in the fledgling American League, that was the number of paying customers the new Chicago White Sox attracted.

The North-South World Series of 1906

When Big Ed Walsh took the mound, the forecast was the same as it was in Seattle—rain all of the time. In the Pacific Northwest, the rain fell from the sky. On the pitching mound, the dampness emanated from Walsh's mouth. His best pitch was the spitball, and when the master of saliva hummed the ball at the batter, it followed the same type of twisty, torturous flight as a bumblebee.

Walsh, who stood 6'1" and weighed 193 pounds, was born in Plains, Pennsylvania, as the youngest of 13 children in 1881, and dropped out of school at age 11 to work in the coal mines. Walsh was a minor character in the White Sox's pitching rotation in 1904 and 1905. In 1906 he learned to throw a spitter, and the fresh moisture added to the ball transformed his career. Walsh's record in 1906 was 17–13. It was the start of a phenomenal seven-year run. In 1908 Walsh had a season for the ages. He won 40 games while losing 15 and pitched 464 innings, the still-standing modern record—for $3,500 in salary. The 40-victory performance is the second highest win total ever. Walsh also pitched a no-hitter during the 1911 season against Boston. When he retired, Walsh owned a 1.82 earned-run average (the best of all time) and in 1946 he was elected to the Baseball Hall of Fame.

The right-hander's breakthrough season coincided with one of the most extraordinary baseball seasons in Chicago history. In 1906 the Cubs finished a dazzling 116–36, still equal to the most wins in major league history. The Cubs won the National League pennant by 20 games.

Meanwhile, the White Sox captured the American League flag with a 93–58 record, though that included an all-time team best winning streak of 19 games. The Sox hit only slightly better than most utility infielders, a startlingly low .230 team batting average. It flabbergasted many that the Sox had been able to eke out the title, and they were labeled "the Hitless Wonders."

The Cubs were heavy favorites to win the World Series. However, in the only all-Chicago World Series ever played, the White Sox upset the Cubs, stunning the North Siders with a mix of low-scoring games and surprisingly timely hitting. The White Sox won the opener 2–1, with the decision going to Nick Altrock, a player who appeared in games during four decades and became known as "the clown prince of baseball" for his baseball humor act.

The Cubs tied the Series by topping the Sox 7–1 in the second game and handling Doc White. The White Sox took Game 3, 3–0, on a shutout thrown by Walsh. Mordecai "Three Finger" Brown, the Cubs' own future Hall of Fame pitcher, shut out the South Siders 1–0 in Game 4. Walsh returned to claim a second victory, 8–6, in Game 5, and the White Sox closed out the Series with an 8–3 triumph in Game 6, White garnering the win. Cubs fans still haven't gotten over the Series loss. And White Sox fans still tease them regularly.

The White Sox victory also had symbolic value. Comiskey and league president Ban Johnson hugged and kissed publicly after the Sox won. Comiskey, belying his later image as a tightwad, contributed his winning Series share to the players' pool.

The White Sox established American League legitimacy in the same manner as the New York Jets did in Super Bowl III by defeating the favored Baltimore Colts 16–7 and proving the staying power of the old American Football League.

The 1906 Series engendered excitement in Chicago, but it was too soon in the developing relationship between the franchises to make it as deep a grudge match as it would be if they met in 2006. The rivalry, for fan allegiance and bragging rights, only intensified, but the two teams have yet to again meet in a World Series. It is widely assumed such an event would paralyze the city of Chicago and that ticket demand for such a Series would set new records.

Given that there was no television or radio at the time, the media hype in the 2-cent newspapers of 1906 was significant. Some newspapers devoted entire pages to the preview of the Series. It was possible to buy bleacher seats for a listed price of 50 cents and box seats for $2, but it was reported that scalpers sought $20 for some tickets and police made arrests of those violating an already-in-place scalping law. Yet freezing weather for Game 1 held attendance to 12,693 at West Side Park.

Trailing three games to two entering the sixth game of the Series was an unaccustomed status for the seemingly unbeatable Cubs. To change their luck, team operators staged an elaborate pregame show. One highlight was the appearance of four live bear cubs on the field. Two were borrowed from the Lincoln Park Zoo. Two came from a local amusement park and were given to the team, though the

White Sox fans hold up a sign reminding everyone in attendance of the Sox's 1906 World Series victory over the Chicago Cubs.

> **DID YOU KNOW . . .** That in 1906 when the White Sox were called "the Hitless Wonders," the team's high average hitter was Frank Isbell, who batted .279, and the team leaders in home runs were Fielder Jones and Billy Sullivan, who each hit just two?

long-term record of their stay with the franchise remains undocumented. Neither the baseball Cubs, nor the furry cubs, could sidetrack the White Sox. In one of the most glorious triumphs in team history, the White Sox aced out the Cubs in the Series.

The season was the beginning of something special for Walsh, whose pitching career ended in 1917 after a draining 1913 arm strain, likely the result of overwork. But the end of his active throwing days did not mark the end of Walsh's baseball involvement. He briefly managed in the minors, spent six seasons between 1923 and 1930 as a coach with the White Sox, and was even employed for the 1922 season as an American League umpire. For one season, he coached a Notre Dame baseball team that included his pitching sons Edward Jr. and Robert. Young Ed Walsh pitched for the White Sox, too, over parts of four seasons, but his career was not nearly as distinguished as his dad's. The second-generation Ed's lifetime record was 11–24.

On June 22 of 1958, a frail Ed Walsh returned to Comiskey Park in a wheelchair for a tribute day. Suffering from arthritis and cancer, Ed Walsh Day marked the final major public appearance of the great hurler. Among the former White Sox greats attending was Walsh's old catcher, Ray Schalk. Walsh was not strong enough to throw out an official first pitch covering 60 feet, 6 inches, but when someone teased him and suggested he toss a spitball to Schalk, Walsh came through. He licked two fingers, gripped the baseball, and threw it five feet to Schalk.

"Ladies and gentlemen, I want to thank you from the bottom of my heart," Walsh told the fans. "This day I'll remember as long as I live." Walsh did not live much longer. He died in May of 1959, only days after his 78th birthday.

TRIVIA

How many times did Big Ed Walsh lead the White Sox in seasonal earned-run average and what was his lowest ERA?

Answers to the trivia questions are on page 173.

TOP 10

White Sox Shutout Leaders

1. Ed Walsh   57
2. Doc White   42
3. Billy Pierce   35
4. Red Faber   29
5. Ed Cicotte   28
6. Ted Lyons   27
7. Jim Scott   26
8. Frank Smith   25
9. Reb Russell   24†
   Wilbur Wood   24†

At least two poems, preserved in the Baseball Hall of Fame Library archives, commemorate Ed Walsh's life and career. A poem written about his out-of-the-limelight, quiet days in the 1940s when a youngster met Walsh as a milk delivery man, won first prize in a *Kansas Quarterly* contest. A much longer poem, titled "The Pitching Master," summarizes Walsh's entire career in rhyme.

A genial man, decades after retirement, Walsh estimated that he had signed 1.5 million autographs. He was still signing them in his wheelchair on Ed Walsh Day.

Comiskey Park

Charles Comiskey might not have been free to place a new ballpark anywhere he wanted because of his agreement with the Cubs, but he was free to build the fanciest ballpark his wallet and ego could handle and his mind could imagine. When Comiskey Park opened its doors for White Sox play in July of 1910 it was indeed the baseball Taj Mahal the owner coveted.

One of the regular catastrophes of early 1900s baseball was the tendency for old wooden stands in ballparks to burn down. The likelihood that a park with wood plank fencing would become firewood was very high. In addition, the magnates of the time were beginning to realize that baseball was a growth business and their home grounds were not large enough. What was the sense of marketing a team into demand when you couldn't supply enough tickets?

Comiskey evaluated the recent past and recognized signs of coming change. And being the Mark Cuban of his day—an individual sports team owner flush with bucks—he proposed building the sturdiest and plushest baseball showplace in the majors. He predicted it would be hailed as "the baseball palace of the world."

When the St. Paul club moved to Chicago, the White Sox took up residence at a wooden stadium at 39th Street and Wentworth. The one-time cricket field held about 8,000 people. For years Comiskey sought an appropriate patch of ground on which to build a much larger team home.

Eventually, Comiskey invested $100,000 in South Side land at the corner of 35th Street and Shields, and construction crews began the heavy lifting in February of 1909. The goal was to build one of the sport's few concrete and steel stadiums by mid-season 1910. The stadium was partially built atop an old junkyard. Many years later, White Sox Hall of Fame shortstop Luke Appling said his spikes clanked against a lump of something protruding into the base path.

"I start digging and digging," he said, "and lo and behold it turns out to be a blue and white coffee pot."

Over the years, Comiskey Park has come to be described as Charles Comiskey's "million-dollar baby," but accounts at the time say that the owner spent $500,000 to get the stadium up and running for its July 1, 1910, debut. Brass bands and a parade highlighted the festivities. The White Sox met the St. Louis Browns that day, but even with Big Ed Walsh on the mound, they were defeated 2–0.

Comiskey did not initially name the new structure after himself. The ballpark was at first called simply White Sox Park. Later in the

A view of the main entrance at the old Comiskey Park in its glory days.

DID YOU KNOW . . . That the 1910 White Sox were the worst hitting team in major league history? The club batted .211, the lowest team average of any in either the American or National League in the 20th century, and was last in the league that season in slugging percentage, home runs, and doubles.

decade, Comiskey's name was appended to it, and the name stuck long after the family ceased affiliation with the team.

White Sox play declined following the 1906 World Series. In 1910 the Sox went 68–85 and finished 35½ games out of first place in the American League standings. The attraction for the club that season was the new stadium, not the product on the field. Comiskey Park was 363 feet down the left- and right-field lines, and in order to hit a home run over dead center, a ball had to travel more than 420 feet. A cannon, rather than a Louisville slugger, would have been useful. A major Comiskey Park distinguishing characteristic was its double-decker seating. From the outside, with white brick and arched windows, the park in its own way resembled a wedding cake.

Owner Comiskey hired Zachary Taylor Davis as the architect for his project and soon after Davis also designed Weegham Park, better known to the world in subsequent years as Wrigley Field. Comiskey was in the forefront of change, jump-starting a period of baseball stadium expansion. Boston's Fenway Park opened in 1912—the same week the *Titanic* sunk. Detroit's Navin Field/Briggs/Tiger Stadium also opened in 1912. And Wrigley came along in 1914.

Not everything was perfect. Comiskey Park was built close enough to Chicago's famous stockyards for its patrons to suffer in the flight path of dramatic aromas on a windy day. Other times, fans had to bundle up in coats to deflect cold breezes. By 1927, partially encouraged by the booming attendance Babe Ruth and the lively ball era ushered in, Comiskey expanded his park by 23,000 seats, making it one of the largest stadiums in the United States.

Over the years, Comiskey Park also hosted Chicago Cardinals National Football League games, heavyweight title fights, and concerts performed by big-name acts from The Beatles to Michael Jackson. Those designated hitters drew very well.

All-Time Old Comiskey Park Crowds

1. 55,555 vs. Minnesota Twins (double header), May 20, 1973
2. 54,215 vs. New York Yankees (double header), July 19, 1953
3. 53,940 vs. New York Yankees (double header), June 8, 1951
4. 53,325 vs. Cleveland Indians (double header), May 15, 1949
5. 53,067 vs. New York Yankees, July 27, 1954
6. 52,712 vs. Chicago Cubs (exhibition), June 25, 1964
7. 52,593 vs. Boston Red Sox (double header), July 12, 1951
8. 52,494 vs. New York Yankees (double header), June 18, 1933
9. 52,054 vs. New York Yankees (double header), June 10, 1951
10. 52,000 (estimated) vs. New York Yankees, May 8, 1927

Nine no-hitters were pitched in Comiskey Park. In 1933 the first major league All-Star Game was played there. In 1959 the Sox hosted World Series games, and in 1960 then-owner Bill Veeck installed his world-famous exploding scoreboard celebrating home-team home runs and victories.

Above all, Comiskey made its mark as a ballpark featuring great plays and great players, from Ed Walsh to Ted Lyons, from Hoyt Wilhelm to Jack McDowell, from Minnie Minoso to Frank Thomas. At various times the White Sox were "the Hitless Wonders," and "the South Side Hit Men."

Unlike both Fenway and Wrigley, admired for their quirky charms, their unusual dimensions, and offbeat nooks and crannies, from the Green Monster to the ivy, Comiskey was a straight man.

"The beauty of Comiskey Park is subtle," wrote White Sox historian Richard Lindberg. "It is perfectly symmetrical. There are no short porches, weird angles or clinging vines. There is excellence in proportion and a calming reassurance that the park looks the same as it did in 1927 when Babe Ruth came calling."

Much baseball history was written at Comiskey Park, but by 1990 much of it was old and some of it best forgotten. Comiskey was the White Sox home park when the team won the 1917 World Series, but also in 1919 when players shamefully failed to play every game on the up-and-up and gave away a World Series in the Black Sox Scandal, professional sports' worst. For later generations of players, as new parks opened and replaced smaller stadiums, Comiskey screamed of the past.

Dave Winfield, the Hall of Fame outfielder whose American League days centered around the Yankees, once said of Comiskey, "It goes back to the old days, the old school—the dugouts, the locker room, when there were hard players."

Charles Comiskey's palace made baseball memories for 80 seasons. The last game in the park was played on September 30, 1990, and the wrecking ball swung and began cracking the old façade on October 1. The following season, the White Sox opened a new ballpark across the street. Everyone called it New Comiskey Park.

The 1917 World Series Champion White Sox

Around Chicago they remember 1917 more for the White Sox than for World War I, and they recall Eddie Collins better than General "Black" Jack Pershing.

Collins was a straight-and-narrow guy on a team full of rowdy characters. He was college educated on a team of high school dropouts. Eddie Collins was not only the brains of the outfit, he could out-run, out-field, and out-hit almost all of his contemporary Sox, too.

And when it came to the most crucial single play in franchise history, when the Sox needed to make a moment to make a memory, Collins did it. He scored the run that gave the White Sox a World Series championship over the New York Giants. In a Hall of Fame career, Collins was the best-hitting second baseman of all-time, but this was his signature play.

It was not for nothing that Eddie Collins's nickname was "Cocky." He was born in 1887 and by 1906 had made his major league debut with the Philadelphia Athletics under the assumed last name of Sullivan, even though he did not graduate from Columbia University (where he had been quarterback on the football team) until 1907. The 5'9", 170-pound fielder became a star with the A's as a member of the club's so-called $100,000 infield, which would probably be a $25 million infield today. During a 25-year career, Collins batted .333 with 3,315 hits and 1,821 runs scored. He was the American League Most Valuable Player for Philadelphia in 1914, and his $50,000 sale to the White Sox stunned baseball, both for the price tag and the transfer. At the time, it was the highest sale price for a baseball player, and Charles Comiskey then signed Collins to a five-

Second baseman Eddie Collins was a formidable competitor both on and off the field.

year, $60,000 contract. The big bucks for Collins amounted to $12,000 a season. There were no Scott Boras–type agents to take up his cause. Collins played in four World Series for Philadelphia and that was an event Comiskey wished to revisit.

The White Sox emerged as a powerhouse in 1917. Collins joined a club with Shoeless Joe Jackson in the outfield, and with Ed "Knuckles" Cicotte (who won 28 games that season) and Urban "Red" Faber on the mound. Collins was the big-ticket acquisition for the infield, joining Buck Weaver at third base, Arnold "Chick" Gandil at first, and Charles "Swede" Risberg at shortstop. The players would have been rich if they got paid by the nickname. It was a terrific summer in Chicago, with the Sox compiling a 100–54 record.

"In my opinion, the greatest team ever assembled was the 1917 White Sox club," Collins said in 1950, "some members of which were later to fully merit infamy." The Black Sox Scandal team, with most of the same players featured on the 1917 champions, lay two years in the future.

The White Sox faced John McGraw's New York Giants in the 1917 Series. McGraw, known as Little Napoleon because of his dictatorial ways, felt it was his divine right to win the National League pennant. The Giants put together a 26-game winning streak in 1916, but the team had been revamped in the off-season and may not have been as good. Most games in the Series were close. The Sox won the opener 2–1 behind Cicotte. More than 32,000 fans turned out at Comiskey Park, something that would have been impossible at the old 39th Street Grounds.

Game 2 was easier. The Sox won 7–2 riding Red Faber, the spitballing Hall of Famer who is one of the greatest pitchers in team history. The Giants won Game 3, 2–0, and Game 4, 5–0. The Sox took the lead three games to two with an 8–5 Game 5 victory. Faber picked up his second Series victory.

Faber also started Game 6 and once again was credited with the victory when the Sox prevailed 4–2. The winning run was scored early, in the fourth inning, under unusual circumstances. Collins led off the Sox fourth with a grounder to Giants third baseman Heinie Zimmerman. Zimmerman grabbed the ball, but threw the ball past first for a two-base error. Shoeless Joe Jackson hit a fly ball to Dave Robertson, who dropped it in right field, sending Collins to third. Happy Felsch grounded to New York pitcher Rube Benton, who, after witnessing consecutive errors, was probably glad to have the ball in his own mitt. However, things turned equally sloppy when Benton sought to eliminate Collins as the lead runner.

Collins appeared trapped off third and put himself into a rundown while Jackson and Felsch scrambled to reach a base safely. Giants catcher Bill Rariden moved too far up the third-base line, so when Benton threw to Zimmerman, Collins was able to zip past the surprised backstop. No Giant was covering home plate, so Zimmerman had no one to throw to in order to nab Collins. The only one standing in the vicinity was home-plate umpire Bill Klem.

TRIVIA

What is the White Sox's longest winning streak and what year did it take place?

Answers to the trivia questions are on page 173.

TOP 10

White Sox All-Time Winningest Pitchers

1. Ted Lyons   260
2. Red Faber   254
3. Ed Walsh   195
4. Billy Pierce   186
5. Wilbur Wood   163
6. Doc White   159
7. Ed Cicotte   156
8. Joel Horlen   113
9. Frank Smith   108
10. Jim Scott   107

Collins ran for home, Zimmerman in pursuit. Collins was faster. Zimmerman leaned forward trying to make a tag, but Collins was safe at home for a 1–0 lead. Zimmerman was unfairly vilified as the villain in the scenario, with some critics unrealistically charging he should have thrown Collins out. "Who the hell was I going to throw the ball to, Klem?" he responded. If Zimmerman deserved to be called a goat, it was for the initial error that put Collins on base.

Chick Gandil then smashed a single to right field, bringing Jackson and Felsch in to score to clinch the Series 3–0. The race to the plate is the best-remembered play of Collins's career. After his quarter-century playing career, Collins coached with the A's and became an executive with the Red Sox for the last 18 years of his life. He died in a Boston hospital at the age of 63.

The player truly the toast of the town after the 1917 Series was Red Faber, winning pitcher in three of the team's four victories. Faber was born in 1888 in Cascade, Iowa, a place that in no way matched his first name of Urban. Faber was signed by the Pittsburgh Pirates after a couple of years matriculating at St. Joseph's College of Dubuque, Iowa, but was the property of the Giants when Comiskey paid $35,000 for his rights, just in time for the White Sox famed world tour of 1914.

IF ONLY . . . Modern medicine had been able to treat Red Faber's sore right arm to get him healthy for the 1919 World Series, he may have been able to rewrite baseball history. If Faber had been in the White Sox rotation, the gambling conspiracy to throw the Series against the Cincinnati Reds would likely not have been hatched. Faber probably would have won a game or two and given the Sox the crown. The fallout from *Eight Men Out* movie fame would have vanished—no Sox players would have been suspended—and the Sox would have remained a contending team. And baseball would not have hired its first all-powerful commissioner, Kenesaw Mountain Landis. At least not then.

Showman that he was, Comiskey wanted to show off his baseball team and in partnership with the Giants, the teams played 44 exhibition games in Japan, Australia, Ceylon, France, Egypt, England, and a few other miscellaneous stops. Faber actually won his first "major league" game in Hong Kong. He showed enough stuff to become a regular in the White Sox rotation. Although the spitball was banned in 1920, presumably on the grounds of grossness, the new baseball law was not retroactive, and any pitcher who depended on the pitch was grandfathered in and allowed to use it until retirement. Faber, one of the 17 pitchers permitted to keep his spitter going, pitched for the White Sox from 1914 to 1933. He did not retire until he was 45, and at that point was the last legal spitball pitcher in the American League.

Faber said he put endless hours into perfecting the spitball. But once mastered, it allowed for longevity.

"I had success with it because I developed control," Faber said. "It took a lot of continual practice, not just when you were warming up for a game. It was something you had to work on between pitching assignments. The spitter is the easiest delivery there is upon the arm."

Overall, Faber won 254 games with a 3.15 earned-run average and topped 20 victories in a season four times. He was 16–13 in 1917 and saved his best ball for the Series. In 1918 Faber was 4–1 before entering the army during World War I. In 1919 Faber finished 11–9, in a season cut short because of an injured right throwing arm. The loss of Faber before the Black Sox Series against the Cincinnati Reds weakened the White Sox pitching staff and enabled gamblers to develop a plot revolving around starters Cicotte and Claude "Lefty" Williams. Later, it was suggested there might not have been a Black Sox Scandal if Faber had been healthy.

"If Faber had been able to work, I'm sure that no situation could have come up," said Hall of Fame catcher Ray Schalk, one of the so-called "clean Sox." Schalk based his 1959 thoughts on what Faber accomplished in the 1917 Series. "He was our hero and would have been in line for much of the work in 1919."

After Faber retired from pitching, he operated a bowling alley and coached for the White Sox from 1946 to 1948. He ultimately became a surveyor. Faber, who was 88 when he died in 1976, lived long enough to enjoy being inducted into the Hall of Fame in 1964.

For all of his triumphs with the White Sox, Faber never had a finer or prouder period than his trio of wins in the 1917 Series. No one, not Faber, Comiskey, or even Nostradamus, could have envisioned the team going 88 more years before winning another championship.

Black Sox

Black socks. Dirty socks. Dirty laundry. The Black Sox Scandal was the most shameful single episode in Major League Baseball history and most likely all professional sport. It was an evocative and provocative name for a tawdry incident that shook America and shook up the game.

Depending whom is to be believed, five, six, seven, eight, or who knows maybe how many more members of the heavily favored American League pennant–winning White Sox conspired with gamblers to throw the 1919 World Series to the Cincinnati Reds.

In a modern era when athletes are among the elite paycheck earners in American society, it is unfathomable how admired professionals found it worthwhile to stifle pride and sell out for a payoff of what turned out to be only a few thousand dollars apiece. At issue for many of the players who felt cheated after the 1917 championship was failure to receive just reward from miserly Charles Comiskey. He held their salaries down, failed to follow through on promised bonuses, teased them with flat champagne in honor of their achievements, and manipulated playing time to prevent some from acquiring the necessary statistics for contract bonus clauses.

At a time when fraternization with gamblers was at an all-time high, the attempt to fix the World Series was the most brazen scheme of all. Gamblers from kingpin Arnold Rothstein to regional influences like Boston's Joseph "Sport" Sullivan, from double-crossing Abe Attel, the former featherweight boxing champion of the world, to small-timers like Bill Burns, a former major league pitcher, weaved a complex web for what history has decreed was eight members of the White Sox.

Manager Kid Gleason said the 1919 White Sox players consti-
tuted the best ballclub he ever saw. The team featured outfielder
Shoeless Joe Jackson and knuckleball pitcher Ed Cicotte, catcher Ray
Schalk, and pitcher Red Faber, all of them at the time on career paths
that would have taken them to the Hall of Fame. Jackson and Cicotte
were considered part of the bunch who betrayed Gleason, Comiskey,
the fans, the city, and the game.

There is little doubt a conspiracy existed. There is controversy
still about who participated in the fix from the start, who advanced
the idea, who played what role in the games, which gamblers kept
their promises to pay and which gamblers siphoned off cash. The
plot unraveled at the seams much like a baseball hit too hard too
many times, yet the ultimate design succeeded. The White Sox—as
much of a sure-thing lock to take the Series from Cincinnati as a

*Knuckleballer Ed
Cicotte was
among those
implicated in the
infamous "Black
Sox" gambling
scandal of 1919.*

TOP 10

All-Time White Sox Leaders Batting Average

1. Joe Jackson .340
2. Eddie Collins .331
3. Carl Reynolds .322
4. Zeke Bonura .317
5. Bibb Falk .315
6. Taffy Wright .312
7. Luke Appling .310†
   Rip Radcliff .310†
9. Frank Thomas .307†
   Magglio Ordonez .307†

banker who knew the combination to his own safe—lost the nine-game Series to the Reds. The players did not obtain nearly the amount of money pledged to them. The players did not always lose the games they cut a deal to lose. Players supposedly in on the fix and "committed" to giving away runs, played exemplary Series. From one game to the next, from one minute to the next, the fix was on, the fix was off, there was confusion over who was making payoffs and who was pocketing profits. Rumors were so rampant of a fix that they were not spoken in whispers, but fairly shouted across crowded barrooms.

Suspicion was strong. Ring Lardner, one of the masterful sports-writing scribes of the age, is portrayed in the movie *Eight Men Out* as walking through the team on a train singing, "I'm forever blowing ballgames" to the tune of "I'm Forever Blowing Bubbles." He really did so. Lardner and newspaperman Hugh Fullerton kept independent scorecards during the Series and compared plays they thought looked fishy.

The fix was bungled, yet the White Sox ultimately fell and some gamblers somewhere made off with thousands and thousands. Slowly, steadily, mostly through the pugnacious efforts of Fullerton, the truth was outed. It took time, but the nasty secret was exposed, reputations were tarnished, and although the players returned to play the 1920 season for the White Sox, finally a grand jury was convened and returned indictments.

A 1920 syndicated piece by Fullerton began this way: "Baseball disgrace, which was climaxed recently when players of the Chicago White Sox, champions of the American League, were indicted on charges of throwing games in the world's series, has been an open secret for ten months. Practically everyone connected with baseball knew that the series in Cincinnati, the first two and the final game especially, was not played honestly."

If so, Cincinnati players did not say so aloud. They claimed they won the title fair and square. Comiskey said he never suspected, either. Pulitzer Prize–winning author Studs Terkel, born in 1912 and a Chicago institution, played the part of Fullerton in the movie. He formed strong opinions about what took place. "Buck Weaver, third baseman, did not take part in it," Terkel said. "He didn't inform on the other guys. The eighth guy kicked out should've been Comiskey. The way he exploited the players, it made them a natural for a guy like Arnold Rothstein."

Confessions were obtained from a guilt-ridden Ed Cicotte and a baffled Shoeless Joe Jackson, an illiterate who signed his name with an X and said he was misled. Although eight players went to trial and all were acquitted, the new commissioner of baseball, Judge Kenesaw Mountain Landis, issued a stern and unwavering ruling. Landis banned all eight players from baseball for life, and long after their deaths, the suspension is in effect. None played organized baseball again. Comiskey was embarrassed and some blamed him for not being forthcoming about his alleged early knowledge of the fix.

White-haired, domineering, usually unsmiling, the iron-willed Landis ruled baseball for a quarter of a century until his death in 1944, but his first pronouncement after the courtroom acquittal is his most memorable. It was his Gettysburg Address, reading in part, "Regardless of the verdict of juries, no player who throws a ballgame;

TRIVIA

During the pennant-winning regular season for the 1919 Black Sox, who led the team in hitting?

Answers to the trivia questions are on page 173.

no player who undertakes or promises to throw a ballgame; no player who sits in a conference with a bunch of crooked players and gamblers, where the ways and means of throwing ballgames are planned and discussed and does not promptly tell his club about it, will ever play professional baseball."

In an effort to clean up a game he felt gamblers were spoiling, and determined to restore public faith, Landis painted all of the characters in the Black Sox mess with the same brush. Shoeless Joe Jackson, Buck Weaver, Swede Risberg, Chick Gandil, Ed Cicotte, Lefty Williams, Happy Felsch, and Fred McMullin were thrown out of the sport. Weaver waged a decades-long crusade to clear his name, claiming he played his best, and even after his death relatives carried on the campaign. Jackson battled equally hard and equally loud to clear his reputation and likewise, the campaign continues more than a half century after his death. In Jackson's case there is even more at stake because an eligible Shoeless Joe would likely become a Hall of Famer.

Cicotte might have found his way to Cooperstown with a 209–148 record at age 36. He is credited with inventing the knuckle-ball, the wacky, floating pitch so hard to tame, won 28 games in 1917 when the Sox captured the Series and won 29 games in 1919. Comiskey promised Cicotte a $10,000 bonus if he won 30 games that season, but then supposedly ordered Gleason not to pitch Cicotte when he came close. It was Cicotte's bitterness over this slight that led to his susceptibility to sell out to the gamblers.

Cicotte never seemed comfortable with his guilt in losing Games 1 and 4, and when the legal squeeze came, he capitulated. Jackson, too, produced a confession of sorts. The players were acquitted after the prosecutor admitted the confessions disappeared. They resurfaced years later and are now part of the historical record. In 1965, when *Detroit Free Press* sports columnist Joe Falls visited Cicotte at his home, Cicotte told him, "I admit I did wrong, but I've paid for it for the past 45 years."

Cicotte, who raised five children and ultimately became a strawberry farmer near Detroit, said he tried to make up for his poor choice. "I don't know of anyone who ever went through life without making a mistake," he said. "Everybody who has ever lived

By the NUMBERS 25—Still in the dead-ball era, during the American League pennant–winning season of 1919, the White Sox were able to win 88 games and advance to the World Series despite hitting so few home runs as a team.

has committed sins of their own. I've tried to make up for it by living as clean a life as I could. I'm proud of the way I've lived and I think my family is, too."

Cicotte died at the age of 84 in 1969.

To some, third baseman Weaver presents the clearest case for innocence. Weaver said he was only guilty of not squealing on his teammates. He batted .324 versus Cincinnati and handled 27 chances at third without an error. Over his nine-year career, Weaver batted .272 and was regarded as one of the best at his position. When the players were indicted, Weaver originally fought for a separate trial, but stuck with the group. In 1922 Weaver petitioned Landis for reinstatement and appeared before him for a private hearing.

Weaver said that when the fix was planned he had just opened a drugstore and needed the $10,000 he was offered to throw games, but said he declined to take the money. He also said he debated telling Comiskey of the bribe offer, but decided to just keep quiet and play his best because he didn't even know how many players were in on the fix. Weaver was 32, still young enough to play. Landis denied the petition.

In 1953—nine years after Landis' death—Weaver, who became a race track paramutual clerk, wrote from Chicago to the commissioner's office asking for reinstatement. Once again he was turned down. George "Buck" Weaver died at the age of 65 in 1956, unable to free himself of the stigma of the Black Sox. At the time, catcher Ray Schalk spoke up for Weaver, his old roommate. He called Weaver "the greatest third baseman I ever saw" and said the Black Sox Scandal "caused Weaver the tortures of hell."

For decades after Weaver died, aging family members worked to clear his name. In 2003, across the street from the All-Star Game at the new Comiskey Park, a rally was held promoting The Buck Weaver Story with the theme "Banned from baseball in 1921, Buck Weaver was no snitch." There has been no change in his status.

Shoeless Joe Jackson played in the majors until he was 31. He compiled a .356 lifetime batting average with the Cleveland Indians and the White Sox. If Jackson's career had not ended abruptly, he likely would have become an early Hall of Famer. Many observers and writers over the years, still aching for the pure truth of the matter, portray Jackson as sympathetically as Weaver.

At the height of the madness, with the city of Chicago rooting for its ballplayers to be cleared, the possibly mythological story surrounding Jackson's encounter with a little boy seemingly summarized the situation. Legend suggests that when exiting the courtroom, Jackson felt a tug on his sleeve from a crying youngster saying, "Say it ain't so, Joe." Jackson reportedly said that sadly, it was so.

The story may be fiction. The incident may be real. But the phrase—"Say it ain't so, Joe"—drifted into the public lexicon and endures. No matter how many years passed, however, the tarnish of the scandal never washed off those it touched.

DID YOU KNOW . . . That before Kenesaw Mountain Landis became the commissioner of baseball for life in 1920, he was a federal judge?

Shoeless Joe

The advertisement featured a picture of Shoeless Joe Jackson and the simple words, "When he wears them." It was a clever endorsement for a particular brand of shoe, making use of the great hitter's euphonious nickname.

There is little dispute that Joe Jackson was one of the best hitters in baseball history, a marvelous fielder with a glove described by some as "the place where triples go to die," and he had the talent of a Hall of Famer. But skill was not the issue in the tale of Joe Jackson, who split his major league playing time among the Philadelphia Athletics, Cleveland Indians, and White Sox.

The story of Joe Jackson is a Shakespearean tragedy. He was born in poverty, had little opportunity to learn his letters, and was forevermore burdened with the label of illiterate. He rose to the heights of the national pastime, then recklessly threw it all away (or was conned into cooperation in illegal deeds) by greedily participating in the Black Sox Scandal (or by being innocently lured in). Exiled from the game he loved by commissioner's edict after a trial that acquitted him and seven other White Sox teammates, Jackson evaporated into the mists, became an ethereal, ghost-like figure. And that was the real Joe Jackson. Returned to prominence by a W. P. Kinsella short story entitled "Shoeless Joe Comes to Iowa" and the subsequent Kevin Costner movie *Field of Dreams*, Jackson the player was introduced to a new generation as a ghost of a character.

Jackson was born in South Carolina in 1889, made his major league debut for five games in 1908 with the Athletics, and five more in 1909, then joined the Indians. In 1911, the season of his first serious action, Jackson batted .408, one of the highest averages of all

Joseph "Shoeless Joe" Jackson was one of the key figures in the Black Sox Scandal, which rocked baseball and created the position of baseball commissioner. Jackson was an outfielder in the major leagues from 1908 to 1920 and posted a lifetime batting average of .356.

time. He was still only 22. Jackson came to the White Sox midway through the 1915 season.

Jackson's family lived in poverty in rural Pickens County near the Blue Ridge Mountains. By age six Jackson swept floors at the nearby Brandon Mill. He had little formal schooling and seemed destined for a mill-working life. As a child he bristled when snooty kids called him "lint head," though he did not take much kindlier to the nickname "Shoeless Joe" when it was first applied in 1908.

By then the sturdy 6'1", 200-pound Jackson was playing in the Carolina Association. One day, as he tells it, new shoes were blistering his feet. Sore from the ordeal, the next day in the field he kicked off his shoes altogether. Jackson said he hit a triple and as he settled onto third base someone yelled from the stands, "You shoeless sonofagun!" Others that day took note of the description, notably a sportswriter named Scoop Latimer, and soon Jackson was called "Shoeless" all around the league.

"I never played barefoot and that was the only day I played in my stockinged feet, but it stuck with me," Jackson said.

Ironically, when he became a major leaguer and could afford a more dapper wardrobe, Jackson filled his closet with fancy leather shoes of various types. He was the Imelda Marcos of the American League.

Jackson got along with his teammates—who had great respect for his ability—but was also sometimes teased because of his lack of smarts. He had his wife Katie read the newspaper to him to keep up with current events, but by all reports was naïve and easily hoodwinked. Joe Williams, a New York sportswriter, calling Jackson "pure country," said he would not have been surprised to learn that Jackson made a down payment on the Brooklyn Bridge.

Just how innocent Jackson was in the Black Sox Scandal is a major controversy. History has portrayed Jackson as someone led astray by more evil teammates. It has been suggested that he did not so much enter into a conspiracy with the players plotting the World Series fix against Cincinnati as he was dragged along through cajoling, silent assent, and an anguish over what to do with all his "friends" in on the deal. Jackson always insisted he played all out, and he hit .375 and made no errors in the Series.

When the players were pursued by the law, Jackson, once again portrayed as naïve in the hands of manipulative attorneys, confessed. The confession disappeared before the Cook County trial, but resurfaced eventually. What to make of his words may depend on the reader's predisposition to think of Jackson as innocent or guilty.

TRIVIA

Who holds the record for most strikeouts by a White Sox pitcher in a single game?

Answers to the trivia questions are on page 173.

In the court document, Jackson did confess to being approached more than once by teammate Chick Gandil to throw the World Series. "He told me that I could take it, or let it go, they were going through with it," Jackson said. He said he told Gandil he would not be part of it, but that Gandil said he was "already into it and I might as well stay in."

All-Century Team

White Sox fans voted for a full team of the century, announced September 30, 2000, marking 100 years of franchise play. Three of the players—Shoeless Joe Jackson, Buck Weaver, and Ed Cicotte—were among the eight banned for life because of the Black Sox Scandal.

Players	Position	Years
Dick Allen	1B	1972–1974
Luis Aparicio	SS	1956–1962, 1968–1970
Luke Appling	SS	1930–1950
Harold Baines	OF	1980–1989, 1996–1997, 2000–2001
Chico Carrasquel	SS	1950–1955
Eddie Collins	2B	1915–26
Carlton Fisk	C	1981–1993
Nellie Fox	2B	1950–1963
Ozzie Guillen	SS	1985–1997
Joe Jackson	OF	1915–1920
Jim Landis	OF	1957–1964
Sherm Lollar	C	1952–1963
Bill Melton	3B	1968–1975
Minnie Minoso	OF	1952–1957, 1960–1961, 1964, 1976, 1980
Ray Schalk	C	1912–1928
Frank Thomas	1B/DH	1990–2005
Robin Ventura	3B	1989–1998
Buck Weaver	3B	1912–1920
Ed Cicotte	P	1912–1920
Red Faber	P	1914–1933
Ted Lyons	P	1923–1942
Gary Peters	P	1959–1969
Billy Pierce	P	1949–1961
Ed Walsh	P	1904–1916
Doc White	P	1903–1913
Hoyt Wilhelm	P	1963–1968
Wilbur Wood	P	1967–1978

Jackson said he took Gandil's response as a threat and said, "I told him any time they wanted to have me knocked off to have me knocked off." He said Gandil just laughed. Jackson told the questioner in his deposition that he at all times ran, hit, fielded, and threw with the intention of winning.

There was much grumbling about short payments among the players as the Series went on, but Jackson admitted pocketing $5,000. In the movie *Eight Men Out*, Jackson is seen lying on a hotel room bed when another player opens his door and tosses an envelope on the bureau. Jackson does not speak.

So disturbed by what swirled around him, Jackson did go to manager Kid Gleason before the World Series began and ask to be benched. However, he did not explain why and he never told owner Charles Comiskey the fix was in. Without a good reason to act otherwise, Gleason kept his best player in the lineup.

Jackson was asked by the prosecutor, "Did you do anything to throw those games?"

"No, sir," he replied.

"Any game in the Series?"

"Not a one," he said. "I didn't have an error or make no misplay."

Jackson said Gandil offered him $10,000 to join the conspiracy, and he said no. Later, Gandil offered $20,000 and Jackson said he turned that down, as well. But when the $5,000 showed up, he kept it.

"Weren't you very much peeved that you only got $5,000 and you expected to get 20?" Jackson was asked for the deposition.

"No," he said. "I was ashamed."

When he was at the top of his game as a spray hitter, Jackson named his bats. The most famous of these was "Black Betsy," a black-hued piece of lumber that was represented as his favorite. There was no denying Jackson's specialness. Babe Ruth modeled his swing after Jackson's.

Baseball meant everything to Jackson—he had been playing for pay since he was 13—and he was blessed with a gift. In 1916 he was making a $10,000 salary and bought a home in Savannah, Georgia. But when he was banned from organized ball, the man with no education and minimal skills who so desperately sought to escape the mills, had few options.

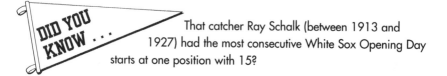

That catcher Ray Schalk (between 1913 and 1927) had the most consecutive White Sox Opening Day starts at one position with 15?

In a much less transparent era, where no TV cameras would find him, Jackson began playing for teams under fake names. For years he continued to play the game he loved in semi-pro leagues not governed by Commissioner Kenesaw Mountain Landis. He was paid $100 a game and played into his forties.

Eventually, Jackson moved to Greenville, South Carolina, ran a liquor store, and helped teach youngsters the game of baseball. In a 1941 interview, Jackson, suffering from a heart condition, said he realized baseball would never reinstate him.

"I've lost hope, Sonny," he told a sportswriter. "That would be a happy day, but it won't come. It's hard to take, but what can a fellow do, especially when he's not going to be around much longer? They cut me off at my prime. I was only 32. But I don't mind that so much as the black mark I'll be taking along with me. I used to hope that they'd clear my name, but I guess they never will. My God, Sonny, that's the hard part."

Jackson went to his grave in 1951, firm in the belief he was officially disgraced forever. The movie *Field of Dreams*—clearly sympathetic to his cause—stirred things up four decades later.

And then, in a speech at a Florida symposium in 1998, Hall of Famer Ted Williams gave new impetus to the Jackson believers who feel he should be made eligible for Hall of Fame voting.

"I want baseball to right an injustice," Williams said. "It's to the memory of one of the greatest hitters, greatest players, who ever played this game. I'm talking about Shoeless Joe Jackson. And it's about time we say he's paid the price, served his sentence—served his sentence for a crime no court of law ever found him guilty of."

Shoeless Joe Jackson long ago had his final say on the Black Sox Scandal. He may never be pardoned, but for six seasons with the team, he was one of the greatest players in Chicago White Sox history.

The Leftover Shambles of a Team

Rather than let the Black Sox Scandal eat away at his stomach like a continuously eroding acid, Ray Schalk sought to bury the bad memory. The long-time White Sox Hall of Fame catcher was regarded as above reproach when the rumors of Sox players involved in a World Series fix burst through the dam of secrecy.

The player known as "Cracker" during his 1912–1928 career with the Sox was one of the honest guys cost a Series title ring because of the nefarious conduct of fellow players. Schalk said he knew nothing of the conspiracy and never suspected it was so widespread.

Various accounts of the tumultuous eight-game Series against the Cincinnati Reds put Schalk at public odds with shortstop Swede Risberg. It was reported that they had a fistfight in the clubhouse when Schalk voiced suspicion about Risberg's play. Schalk said such a fight never occurred, but that he sarcastically commented on Risberg's efforts.

"As a matter of fact, I did challenge Risberg verbally early in the Series," Schalk said, "but it was the same kind of criticism that many players give their teammates for bad plays in the heat of battle. I told Risberg what I thought of some of his plays, but I did not charge him at the time with trying to toss the game."

Schalk played 1,762 major league games while batting .253 and acting as a take-charge field leader. He was the rock for the White Sox pitching staff and, after the scandal, the rock of a humiliated, down-trodden franchise.

Stripped of much their talent after their forced housecleaning, the White Sox needed reinforcements. Shaken by the betrayal and at-best discomfited by how close he came to bearing some blame for it, Charles Comiskey had to rebuild in a hurry.

The Roaring '20s were one of the country's most frivolous periods and in the American League marked the rise of the New York Yankees, superstar Babe Ruth, and the home run as a major offensive weapon. But the 1920s were horrible for the White Sox. Al Capone, Jack Dempsey, and Red Grange were only a few people who enjoyed a more prosperous decade than the White Sox.

Pretty much only the end-of-decade stock market crash was comparable to the White Sox plight. Overnight the Sox went from the best in the world to one of the worst in the majors. In 1921, the year after the eight Black Sox were banished, the White Sox finished 62–92. The team did not have a winning record again until 1925, and even then was just four games over .500.

Ray Schalk, shown in the 1950s modeling a new catcher's glove to handle knuckleballers, was the franchise's rock throughout the Black Sox Scandal and its aftermath.

Eddie Collins was running the show then. In 1926, with an 81–72 finish, it appeared the club's fortunes had turned. But the worst was yet to come. Not only did the White Sox not have another winning season in Comiskey's lifetime (he died in 1931), they did not break .500 again until 1936.

The drastic punishment of the eight players ended careers dramatically but also ruined the franchise for years. As time passed, and the White Sox remained stalled in the nether regions of the American League, some began to call their fate "The Curse of the Black Sox Scandal." Certainly in the beginning the label was deserved and accurate. After that? It took the White Sox 40 years from 1919—until the last member of the Comiskey family surrendered majority interest in the team—to win another pennant.

TRIVIA

Who was the first White Sox player to hit three home runs in one game and in what year did he do it?

Answers to the trivia questions are on page 173.

The loss of the players did create opportunity for newcomers. Charlie Robertson was a right-handed throwing Texan who tried to make the big club in 1917 and 1918, but couldn't cut it. In 1922, however, he made the team, and on April 30, pitching against the Detroit Tigers at Navin Field before 25,000 fans who spilled onto the diamond, he threw a perfect game.

Twenty-seven men up and 27 men down in the rare feat. The frustrated Tigers hollered that Robertson threw an illegal pitch, somehow wetting or cutting the ball. Umpire Billy Evans and Tiger outfielder Ty Cobb did everything but strip search Robertson without finding an illegal substance. The White Sox won 2–0.

Robertson finished 14–15 that season, never had a winning year, and when he left the majors in 1928, his lifetime mark was 49–80. He was a supernova who burned brightly in the sky for only the shortest of times, producing a miracle of the moment, not long-term dependability.

Schalk caught the only White Sox perfect game in history and said the Tigers hit only one ball really hard that day, testing Johnny Mostil in left field because of the overflow crowd. "Johnny Mostil nailed [it] while fighting off spectators and mounted police," Schalk said.

One of the Sox 1920s fresh faces who did some outstanding things was outfielder Carl Reynolds. Reynolds played for the team only between 1927 and 1931 after emerging from Southwestern University in Texas, but he had a .322 lifetime Sox average. Despite hitting .359 in 1930—the fifth best in team history—Reynolds today is less known among Sox fans than R. J. Reynolds Tobacco.

The 1920s were a lost decade for the White Sox. The exile of the Black Sox was fresh, players Comiskey bought for $200,000 to fill the holes were not as good, and newspapermen tried to link Comiskey more directly to the scandal. Except for Robertson's one-in-a-million game, the brightest part of the '20s was the signing of pitcher Ted Lyons.

By the numbers and in longevity, Lyons became the greatest pitcher in White Sox history. He played for Baylor University, and Schalk met Lyons in Waco, Texas, in 1923. White Sox pitchers and catchers were participating in a March pre–spring training camp in Texas, and some Sox players and officials toured the small Baylor campus. Schalk agreed to pose for publicity pictures by catching a Baylor pitcher. Schalk said after just four of Lyons's offerings, he knew Lyons was the real deal. Within a week, the 5'11", 200-pound hurler was a member of the White Sox organization, where he stayed for the next 21 years. Lyons had planned to become a lawyer, but stayed a baseball man until 1966.

"I'll never regret making that trip to Waco," said Schalk, who became the White Sox manager in 1927.

It was never easy for Ted Lyons with the White Sox. He often lacked run support and won 260 big-league ballgames while playing for mostly bad teams. Years later, one *New York Times* writer called Lyons's teammates "a gosh-awful collection of humpty-dumpties." Lyons's White Sox never won a pennant, never played in a World

By the NUMBERS

4—Uniform number worn by Hall of Fame shortstop Luke Appling between 1930 and 1950 for the Sox. Teams did not begin putting numbers on the backs of their uniforms until the Yankees did so in the 1920s. Appling's No. 4 is the oldest retired White Sox number.

TOP 10

Most White Sox Games Pitched

	Player	No. of Games
1.	Red Faber	669
2.	Ted Lyons	594
3.	Wilbur Wood	578
4.	Billy Pierce	456
5.	Ed Walsh	426
6.	Bobby Thigpen	424
7.	Hoyt Wilhelm	361
8.	Doc White	360
9.	Ed Cicotte	353
10.	Keith Foulke	346

Series. As long as his career was—and he wore the uniform as an active player until 1946, except for World War II time off—Lyons's performances were sandwiched between White Sox good times.

Few players have toiled so honestly with such little team reward. In Chicago, Lyons's career parallels Ernie Banks's, the great Cubs hitter who never saw a World Series from any perch besides the stands or on TV.

Lyons was regarded as a personable player who never felt his longevity was that special. Most of his greatest mound achievements occurred in the 1920s. He took a no-hitter as far as two outs in the ninth inning during a 1925 game against the Washington Senators, but couldn't put a third strike past pinch-hitter Bobby Veach.

"I had Washington shut out with two out in the ninth," said Lyons, who shook off his catcher's sign and threw a curve instead of a fastball that Veach cracked for a single.

In 1926 Lyons did throw a no-hitter against the Red Sox. He won 22 games that season and the same amount in 1930, and he won 21 in 1925. But even in his best years, Lyons suffered double-digit losses for a failing team and he lost 230 games in his career. He was often spied throwing chairs in the locker room after a tough defeat.

DID YOU KNOW ... That seven White Sox players played professional football? Most competed in the 1920s and 1930s. The most famous was Bo Jackson, the Sox outfielder and star Raiders running back.

Lyons, a switch-hitter who occasionally pinch-hit, had to be creative to remain a mainstay of the Sox after 1931 when an injured pitching arm cost speed on his fastball. Lyons developed a knuckleball that put less strain on his arm and began an entirely new phase of his career.

In the early 1920s, before Lyons's prowess with a bat was recognized, manager Eddie Collins pinch-hit for him. Lyons liked to tell a story that summarizes both pride in his hitting and his humorous bent. Years later, Lyons tweaked Collins with the tale of the time he traveled to Joliet, south of Chicago, to participate in an exhibition game against a prison team.

"They've got a short left field there," Lyons said. "After I slammed four doubles against the bricks, the warden asked me not to come back—seems he was afraid I'd knock the wall down and there'd be a break."

Lyons never pitched for a White Sox team that placed higher than third, and in the latter stages of his career, manager Jimmy Dykes made him a "Sunday" pitcher. Lyons remained a once-a-week drawing card from 1939 through 1942. If his stamina was failing, Lyons seemed far from washed up in those stints.

During the 1940 season, the White Sox held a Ted Lyons Day. There were 40,000 spectators as Lyons received an automobile, clothing, and hunting guns. Then he went out and beat the Red Sox.

In 1942 Lyons started 20 games for the White Sox and pitched a complete game in every one, winning 14. Lyons always had marvelous control, and in 1939 he pitched 42 innings without allowing a base on balls.

Lyons volunteered for the Marines in 1942. He was just shy of 42 years old and served three years of combat duty. When he returned from the service in 1946, Lyons pitched five games for the White Sox, going 1–4. That season he took over as White Sox manager and led the club for three campaigns. Alas, they were still losers.

Lyons coached for the Detroit Tigers from 1949 to 1953 and for the Brooklyn Dodgers in 1954. He rejoined the White Sox to scout from 1955 to 1966, but when he left the club that time, the lifelong bachelor returned to his original home of Louisiana and managed a rice plantation with his sister until his death in 1986. Before that, however, in 1955, Lyons was elected to the Hall of Fame.

Tris Speaker, the graceful center fielder for the Indians and Red Sox, said if he was a manager with the pennant on the line, he knew whom he wanted on the mound.

"My choice would be Lyons," Speaker said.

Lyons was the White Sox's and the people's choice for two decades in Chicago.

The Forgettable '30s

The U.S. economy wasn't the only thing in a Depression during the 1930s. South Side baseball fans spent entire summers looking for any tiny thing to cure them of their depression. Usually, they struck out and could only say, "Wait till next year."

During the post-scandal 1920s and for the first six seasons of the 1930s, the White Sox were worse than the Tampa Bay Devil Rays. They may have washed their Sox, but the grime lingered. They were no better than Charlie Brown's hapless *Peanuts* team, going 62–92 in 1930, 56–97 in 1931, 49–102 in 1932, 67–83 in 1933, 53–99 in 1934, and 74–78 in 1935.

It was easier to obtain a drink in an illegal speakeasy during Prohibition than it was for the Sox to put together a winning streak during this period. Enduring highlights were rare, though Carl Reynolds, on July 2, 1930, became the first White Sox player to hit three home runs in a single game against the New York Yankees.

That season was notable, too, for the debut of shortstop Luke Appling. One of the longest-serving and best White Sox players of all time, Appling remained in a Chicago uniform until 1950. Appling, from High Point, North Carolina, was young (23) and naïve when he broke into the majors. He admitted being a hick and said it took time to wear some of the country off his overalls.

"One time I was up there and hit the ball to right-center," Appling said of an at-bat. "It bounced off the fence and I rounded first base. Now, a country boy, you can pull anything on them. The first baseman hollered, 'Come back here!' So I turned around and went back to first instead of getting a double."

IF ONLY . . . Right-handed pitcher Monty Stratton had not gone rabbit hunting at the end of the 1938 season when the pistol he was carrying went off and ended his major league career. Stratton had established himself as a first-rate starter just at a time under new manager Jimmy Dykes when the White Sox were emerging from 15 years of futility with an improving team. Stratton's loss was a fresh setback.

Moe Berg, the brainy catcher who became better known later as an undercover spy for the United States than he ever was as a ballplayer, despite playing parts of 15 major league seasons, seemed to have an interesting pen pal relationship with Sox owner Charles Comiskey dating back to 1926. Berg wanted to play ball, but he also wished to complete his law studies at Columbia University. Given the fact that Berg was fluent in several languages and later became more adept at helping his country than he ever was hitting a fastball, the player's insistence on choosing education over spring training that year was probably wise.

Berg was born in New York in 1902, and he sneaked into the Brooklyn lineup in 1923 for 49 games. In a letter dated January 28, 1926, Comiskey wanted to be sure Berg showed up for spring training and provided him with some career advice.

"Since writing you some time ago, I have given the matter of your reporting for spring training further consideration and feel if you intend remaining in professional baseball that the present time is absolutely the time for you to determine [it] regarding your baseball ability," Comiskey wrote, "as you will be given a thoro [sic] tryout in your position...

"I am giving you this information absolutely for your best welfare and interests as the matter of your college education should be secondary if you intend to make baseball your profession. You should easily be able to convince yourself regarding your ability as a major league player this year and can then determine and map out just what you intend to do in the future."

Berg, who some suggest may have been the smartest man to ever play major league ball, played 41 games for the White Sox in 1926

By the
NUMBERS
12—In 1915 the White Sox defeated the St. Louis Browns all dozen times they faced the visitors in Chicago. It is the best home or road sweep record in a single season in team history.

and remained associated with the team through 1930 even if it seemed to be an uneasy adventure.

On March 5, 1927, Comiskey again wrote to Berg about his education, with a dramatically different tone.

"I am in receipt of your letter of March 3 and was very pleased to hear from you and to note that you desire to remain in school until the latter part of May," Comiskey said. "If this is your wish, then you have my permission to do so, as I would not want to interfere with what you deem is your future interests at this time.

"I would suggest for your own benefit that you endeavor to work out in morning practice with the New York clubs, as either one will be at home all the time you are in school. In this way you will get the benefit of major league pitching and no doubt both clubs will be glad to let you work with them during their practice time."

Berg, basically a backup his entire career, whose lifetime average was .243, ended up with Cleveland in 1931 and split his remaining years in the majors between the Indians, the Senators, and the Red Sox. One of the running jokes about Berg was that he could speak a dozen languages, but couldn't hit in any of them. Playing at a time when many ballplayers admitted to hardly ever cracking a book, Berg was an anomaly. Just how unusual a man and well-rounded a person he was did not become known until much later when the world learned Berg had been a World War II spy for the OSS (the forerunner of the CIA) and produced valuable information for U.S. intelligence on Nazi scientists.

The biggest upheaval for the White Sox in the 1930s came with the death of founder and owner Comiskey, who died in October of 1931. Comiskey was at his summer home in Eagle River, Wisconsin, when he passed away at age 72 on October 26. Rising through the ranks from player to manager to owner, Comiskey was a singular figure in the game. His image took a beating following the Black Sox Scandal, and he had generally withdrawn from public view because of ill health. But "the Old Roman" was popular enough at the time of his death for his body to lie in state for two days in Chicago before the funeral.

American League President Will Harridge said, "Mr. Comiskey was one of the founders of the American League and he fought shoulder to shoulder with Ban Johnson for clean baseball. He made a legion of friends throughout the baseball world, all of whom mourned his passing. His death is a personal loss to me, as he was a true and loyal friend at all times."

The Baseball Hall of Fame did not exist during Comiskey's lifetime, but he was elected in 1939 for all-around contributions to the game.

Control of the White Sox passed to J. Louis Comiskey, Charles's son, though long-time friend and business manager Harry Grabiner played a huge role in running the team for decades, and Grace Comiskey, Louis's widow, took over as chief operator in 1939.

If the White Sox were beginning to feel jinxed by the curse of the Black Sox Scandal, the case of Monty Stratton buttressed the argument.

Monty Stratton first made an appearance in a White Sox box score in 1934—he played just one game. A right-handed pitcher, Stratton, who was from Celeste, Texas, got few more mound opportunities in 1935, but was 5–7 in 1936. By 1937 the 6'5" Stratton had matured into a 200-pounder, becoming a key member of the White Sox staff. He went 15–5 with a 2.40 earned-run average. A year later he was 15–9. Only 26, Stratton figured to have a bright future in the rotation and seemed to be a crucial cog in lifting the team out of its decade-and-a-half-long malaise.

TRIVIA

What are the most .300 hitters the White Sox have had in a season (with a minimum of 300 at-bats), and in how many seasons did they produce them?

Answers to the trivia questions are on page 173.

In early autumn of 1938, shortly after the end of the baseball season, Stratton was hunting rabbits on his mother's farm in Greenville, Texas, when he slipped. As Stratton fell a pistol worn on

DID YOU KNOW ... That White Sox players are the major characters in at least three acclaimed baseball movies—*Field of Dreams, Eight Men Out,* and *The Stratton Story?*

his hip discharged a bullet into his right leg. The shot tore through an artery behind his knee, and Stratton lay in the brush hemorrhaging. He hauled himself slowly back toward the farm house until family members found him. Stratton lost a considerable amount of blood and needed two tranfusions from his brothers. Stratton was weak and severely damaged, and doctors chose to amputate his right leg at the knee because they felt it was the best way to save his life.

Stratton's promise as a leading American League pitcher evaporated the instant the gun went off, but he refused to give up on baseball. Stratton was determined to make a unique comeback, pitching in the majors with a wooden leg. He had that in mind when he reported to the White Sox for the 1939 season, officially as a coach.

On May 1 of that season, the White Sox played an exhibition game against the Chicago Cubs as a benefit for Stratton. The game raised $28,000 from the crowd of 25,594 that watched a 4–1 White Sox win.

Stratton spent three seasons as a Sox coach, never giving up hope that he would regain enough velocity on his fastball, balance in his fielding, or earn enough faith from the team to be given a start. But it didn't happen. However, in an inspiring comeback, four years after the accident, Stratton began pitching again in the minors.

He signed with Lubbock in the West Texas–New Mexico League in 1942. In his first professional work since 1938, Stratton surrendered three hits and two runs, but was not discouraged.

"I was mighty nervous," Stratton said. "But that first inning wasn't as bad as I thought it would be. I just have to learn all over again how to pitch on an artificial leg."

Stratton pitched nine undistinguished innings that season, but made progress, practicing a new windup and delivery. When World War II began, the minors near Stratton's home closed up shop and he did not get another chance to pitch until 1946 when he took the mound for the Class C Sherman Twins of the East Texas League.

Stratton won his first start. Unfortunately, when he slashed a hard shot to center and began running to first, Stratton's artificial leg gave way. Stratton was crawling toward first base when thrown out. Later in the season, Stratton pitched a one-hitter after holding Greenville hitless into the seventh inning.

Amazingly, he won 18 games that season. In 1947, pitching for Class B Waco, Stratton finished 7–7. He pitched periodically for Texas minor league teams until 1953. The story of his return from the accident inspired Hollywood. In 1948 the movie *The Stratton Story* was released with Jimmy Stewart playing Stratton and June Allyson playing his wife, Ethel. The screenplay won an Academy Award for writer Douglas Morrow.

In a goodwill gesture, the Philadelphia Phillies invited Stratton (who died in 1982 after a fresh career raising cattle in Texas) to participate in an old-timers exhibition in 1971 before a game against the Dodgers. It had been more than three decades since Stratton's accident, but baseball still remembered him.

A Group of Stars Brighter Than Hollywood's

Arch Ward was the P. T. Barnum of the sports world, a marketing genius before people knew there was a kind of marketing that didn't involve buying peaches and oranges at a store.

Ward was the sports editor of the *Chicago Tribune* in the 1930s when he dreamed up the idea of inviting all of baseball's best players to town in the middle of the season for a showy exhibition game that would take place concurrently with the World's Fair. Originally Commissioner Kenesaw Mountain Landis and the owners did not want to interrupt the regular season for an exhibition game and the players didn't want to play for free. But Ward was persuasive in telling them what was for their own good, and the major league All-Star Game was born.

The first All-Star Game took place in Chicago, at Comiskey Park, in 1933, and it became the prototype not only for an annual baseball showcase, but for all major professional sports leagues in the United States. Over the years, pro football, pro basketball, hockey, and college football modeled all-star contests after baseball's wildly successful game.

Not every sportswriter gets the opportunity to cover an event that he invented, but Ward jump-started the game, promoted it in his pages, and wrote about it when it took place. The one bad thing for the White Sox was that the team had few players worthy of All-Star designation. The debut All-Star Game occurred during the team's decade of despair, and it was hard to argue many White Sox into the event when the players were preoccupied with hitting poorly, throwing wildly, and losing often.

It was Arch Ward's idea to have a baseball all-star game while Chicago hosted the 1933 World's Fair. This is a view from the top of the fair's sky ride that looks south over the vast expanse of concessions and exhibition buildings.

With 50,000 seats, Comiskey Park, Charles Comiskey's old baseball palace, was a logical staging ground. The inaugural All-Star Game was conceived as a one-time event, not something that was expected to evolve into an annual institution. But the baseball establishment got a quick lesson on the popularity of the contest when bleacher seats sold out 40 minutes after they were made available. And that's without Ticketmaster and relentless telephone busy signals. In a sight that would become commonplace for Rolling Stones tickets and the World Series in the future, some fans waited outside Comiskey's gates all night long for their chance to buy.

It didn't hurt any that the idea man, Ward, took to calling the matchup between American League and National League All-Stars the "Game of the Century." The moniker caught on and the hype machine rolled along faster than the then-popular Packard Twin Six Convertible Coupe—93 miles per hour max—could negotiate the roads.

By the
NUMBERS
6—The number of White Sox pitchers who have earned a victory in the All-Star Game. Edgar Smith, 1941; Early Wynn, 1958; Ray Herbert, 1962; Jack McDowell, 1993; James Baldwin, 2000; Mark Buehrle, 2005

Owners made a few fan-friendly decisions. They decreed that no standing room would be available (capping sales of tickets priced from 55 cents to $1.65 at just over 49,000) to keep the park from becoming too crowded, and that fans could elect the players for the game. For critics who more than 70 years later groan when fans seem to pick the wrong starters based on popularity rather than present-season achievement, well, it started way back when, right from the beginning. Also, right from the start of the July 6, 1933, game, players wore their own team uniforms rather than a league uniform.

Eighteen-man rosters were selected. More than 500,000 fans voted in a nationwide poll to send their favorites to Comiskey. New York Giants manager John McGraw was designated to run the National League squad and Philadelphia Athletics manager Connie Mack supervised the American League team.

There was an All-Star cast worthy of a Hollywood epic credit list. Although the All-Star Game predated the Baseball Hall of Fame, ultimately 17 of the players involved in the 1933 contest, plus both managers, were elected to the hall.

The American League team included the Yankees' Lou Gehrig and Babe Ruth, and the A's Jimmie Foxx and Lefty Grove. The White Sox were represented by infielder Jimmy Dykes and outfielder Al Simmons.

Among the big names from the National League were the Giants' Bill Terry, the Pirates' Paul Waner and Pie Traynor, the Cardinals' Frankie Frisch, and the Cubs' Gabby Hartnett.

Dykes scored the first run in All-Star Game history in the home half of the second inning when pitcher Lefty Gomez drove him in (there was no designated hitter in those days). The biggest star in the American League's 4–2 triumph was Babe Ruth, who hit a two-run homer for the winning runs.

By modern standards—with home-run contests and other glitzy sideshows—the first game had more sedate trappings. AL shortstop

Joe Cronin, later a manager and general manager, remembers the game as being low-key to a degree.

"There were no special luncheons or awards to be given out to the player who got the most votes," he said. "The game had humble beginnings. We all thought this would be the one-and-only All-Star Game, too."

Rather than fade away as a one-year curiosity, the All-Star Game became entrenched because both players and fans wanted to see more. Long before interleague play, players were anxious to establish league supremacy in more ways than just the season-ending World Series. For decades, the game has been a measuring stick of that type.

The historic game established Chicago and Comiskey as the birthplace of the All-Star Game, and while the designation is not as easily recalled by the casual fan, it has retained its links.

The 1950 game was played at Comiskey, too, with the National League winning 4–3 on a 14th-inning home run by Cardinals' second baseman Red Schoendienst. The victory was notable, but not unprecedented—the AL had won 12 of the first 16 games.

Even as it rotates the All-Star Game from town to town, emphasizing showing off new ballparks, Major League Baseball has rewarded Chicago and Comiskey with the game for special anniversaries.

TRIVIA

How many players competed in the All-Star Game for the American League in the 1983 contest at Comiskey Park? How many of them were members of the White Sox?

Answers to the trivia questions are on page 173.

A major celebration was observed for the 50th anniversary game in 1983 at Comiskey. Forty-two living Hall of Famers accepted invitations, and a vast array of former All-Stars competed in an old-timers all-star game. Thirteen of the 15 still-living players who participated in the 1933 game also accepted invitations. The first Negro Leagues East-West All-Star Game, also conducted in 1933 at Comiskey Park, was recognized, and Hall of Famers Cool Papa Bell, Judy Johnson, and Willie Wells joined the festivities.

DID YOU KNOW . . . That little-remembered White Sox players Mike Kreevich, 1938; Thurman Tucker, Orval Grove, 1944; Joe Haynes, 1948; and Cass Michaels, 1949, all represented the team in the All-Star Game?

Luis Aparicio, Luke Appling, Larry Doby, Al Lopez, Billy Pierce, Hoyt Wilhelm, and Early Wynn were just some of the players with White Sox ties who participated in probably the grandest of all All-Star celebrations.

Once again Chicago and Comiskey Park were honored with an All-Star Game in 2003, the 70th anniversary of the first game. *Chicago Tribune* sports columnist Mike Downey joked that one thing that separated that game from the first game was a Viagra billboard. Safe bet. The city celebrated by displaying six-foot-tall, multi-colored bobblehead-like statues of different teams on sidewalks throughout the downtown area. (Probably a shortage of bobblehead dolls in 1933, too.)

A nifty by-product was the choice of White Sox pitcher Esteban Loaiza to start the game. Loaiza was off to the best seasonal start of his life, with an 11–5 record and a 2.21 earned-run average, and was thrilled.

"I could not have imagined this," said Loaiza, who did not know that he would open until a couple of days before the game. "I said, 'Excuse me?' I had my mouth open."

The American League won 7–6. Loaiza didn't figure in the decision, and he wasn't around the White Sox much longer, either. But overall, the extravaganza was a success.

Yes, Chicago, There Is a Future

The man hired to put his finger in the dike and stop the flooding was Jimmy Dykes.

A good ballplayer and a good leader who had a sense of humor and sometimes a sense of the absurd, Dykes became White Sox manager during the 1934 season. Although the Sox fell four games shy of .500 in Dykes's first complete season of 1935, they were in first place on May 28, the latest they occupied that spot in 15 years. In 1936 the Sox did put together a winning season.

Dykes was a fiery, old-time ballplayer born in 1896 in Philadelphia, and he made his major league debut with the Athletics in 1918. His father, James Sr., worked as a watchman for the Phillies. Dykes joined the White Sox as a third baseman in 1933 and played the last seven of his 22 seasons in Chicago, mostly as player-manager. He batted .280 lifetime and drove in more than 1,000 runs.

The 5'9", hard-nosed player was a cigar-smoking big talker who liked to tell stories and loved to win. He could be loud, profane, and funny. Once, in the middle of a 10-day slump, Dykes said, "I guess I'm the All-American out."

Dykes's personality woke players up during his 1934–1946 managerial tenure—the longest in team history. As a player, Dykes had been a hell-raiser. On an infamous occasion, he was shot with a pistol wielded by a troubled ex-girlfriend but refused to press charges.

Lou Comiskey acquired Dykes, slugging outfielder Al Simmons, and Mule Haas in a $125,000 deal with the A's, and it proved a smart one for the White Sox, especially after Dykes became the team's ninth manager in 14 seasons.

Long after retiring from baseball, Dykes said that when he was a beginning manager, he was too impatient with his starting pitchers and yanked them too quickly. Once, when he trekked to the mound to remove White Sox hurler Bill Dietrich, the pitcher grew so angry that, rather than hand the game ball to the boss, he heaved it over the grandstand roof.

"That is the best throw you've made today," Dykes said. "It's costing you a hundred bucks."

Dykes was known for his candor with umpires. Dykes, who had as many facial expressions as Casey Stengel, and talked nearly as good a game, wrote a magazine article with the headline, "Some of My Best Friends Are Umpires." Part of the lead paragraph read as follows: "Some fellows, who haven't the same deep affection for umpires that I have, just let them go on missing strikes and close plays on the bases, calling fair balls foul and vice versa. I couldn't do that to a friend. When I notice one of my best friends, who happens to be an umpire, acting blind behind the plate, I can't help telling him about it."

The White Sox had been rebuilding since the Black Sox Scandal, and as the new decade turned, the team accumulated talent. Luke Appling took over as shortstop in 1930 and began a 20-year Hall of Fame run. Al Simmons, already an All-Star left fielder with the A's, was sold to the White Sox with Dykes and anchored an outfield spot for four years.

Aloysius Harry Szymanski, also known as "Bucketfoot," was born in 1902 in Milwaukee to Polish immigrants, and changed his last name to Simmons as he made his way into the majors in 1924 with the A's. Simmons played in the American League for 20 years and became one

DID YOU KNOW . . . That the White Sox received their only two no-hitters over a three-decade period from pitchers in the 1930s who in a combined 15 seasons for the team had just one truly outstanding year? Vern Kennedy pitched a no-hitter against the Cleveland Indians in 1935. (Kennedy was 21–9 in 1936.) Bill Dietrich pitched a no-hitter against the St. Louis Browns in 1937. (He was 10–6 in 1940.)

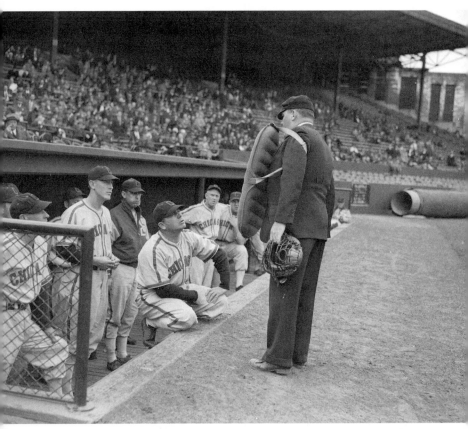

Umpire Bill Summers has a few words with scrappy manager Jimmy Dykes, kneeling in the dugout, after Dykes heckled Boston Red Sox rookie pitcher Herb Hash on May 1, 1940.

of the game's greatest hitters. He retired with a lifetime batting average of .334, won two AL batting championships, and he drove in 1,827 runs in his Hall of Fame career. Simmons gained early attention for his odd batting stance, pointing his left foot straight toward third base. While he was tempted to alter it, A's manager Connie Mack left Simmons alone. Simmons ended up bettering .300 14 times. Mack was restructuring his finances when he sold Simmons to Chicago, where he batted .331 in 1933 and .344 in 1934.

Simmons was enthused over his fresh start, and it was observed that the well-established hitter played with the zest of a rookie.

TOP 10

White Sox Longest Losing Streaks

	Time Span of Losing Streak	No. of Games Lost
1.	August 9–26, 1924	13
2.	September 10–22, 1927	12
3.	July 7–18, 1956	11t
	September 14–24, 1921	11t
	July 9–20, 1910	11t
6.	June 11–20, 1976	10t
	April 10–25, 1968	10t
	May 26–June 4, 1938	10t
	September 17–26, 1934	10t
	August 7–19, 1932	10t
	September 14–22, 1931	10t

"I act like a rookie because I feel like one," Simmons said. "I'm starting all over again. I've taken the slant that what I did in Philadelphia doesn't count now. It's what I do in Chicago. I used to hear people say that change of scenery was good for a ballplayer, but I thought it was bunk."

Bucketfoot's hitting style made managers edgy, but he survived all well-intentioned advice to maintain his style.

"That's the natural way for me to hit," Simmons said. "What if I do pull away from the plate? Suppose I do put my left foot in the water bucket? I get my power from my arms and wrists."

When Simmons slumped, losing nearly 70 percentage points off his batting average in 1935, the White Sox benched him and then shipped him to the Detroit Tigers for $70,000. If you hit .344, you can plant one foot in Lake Michigan, but if you hit .267, suddenly that water bucket looks deeper than the Atlantic Ocean.

The White Sox probably gave up on Simmons too soon since he played nine more seasons, though he never matched his best batting averages again, either. Simmons, who after retirement coached for the Cleveland Indians and ran a baseball school in New York, was elected to the Hall of Fame in 1953. However, he died suddenly of a heart attack only a few years later at age 54, collapsing on a Milwaukee street.

Simmons was a transition player for the White Sox, a big name who could perform great feats as Dykes gradually rebuilt the worst team in the game into one he believed could win a pennant. In 1936, when the Sox became winners again with an 81–70 season, Dykes counted on a different crew of hitters.

Dykes had the always-reliable Appling, who had the best year of his career, hitting a team-record .388; Zeke Bonura, who batted .330 with 138 runs batted in; Ray "Rip" Radcliff, who batted .335; and Mike Kreevich, who hit .307. Once laughingstocks, the White Sox were again taken seriously. To a point. Dykes loved the pop in Bonura's bat, but he was brutally honest about Bonura's stone-footed navigation in the field.

From 1934 to 1937, Bonura, whose nickname was "Bananas," was the White Sox first baseman. He almost always hit .300 or higher, and he was adept at scooping up grounders hit to him. The ones that got away were the balls hit a few feet this way or that way.

"He was unable to use his feet, except for standing," Dykes said.

Dykes was the kind of heady player who accomplished as much on the diamond with his brains as his physical tools, so when a guy like Bonura came along who could powder the ball, but lacked in the game's finer points, it drove the manager wacky. To Bananas, learning the White Sox signs was tougher than scoring an 800 on the math SATs. Once Dykes flashed Bonura the bunt sign repeatedly because it was apparent he was confused. Finally, the field boss simply shouted, "Bunt!" While the action certainly tipped off the opposing team, Bonura did make a perfect sacrifice bunt.

"I lay down on the bench and sobbed," Dykes said.

Bonura was traded to Washington, and the first time the White Sox played the Senators, a Chicago coach urged Dykes to change the team signs since Bonura was aware of them.

"He didn't know 'em when he was with us," Dykes responded. "Why should we change 'em now?"

Dykes desperately wanted to bring White Sox Nation its first pennant since the 1919 Black Sox Scandal and its first World Series

IF ONLY . . . The White Sox held off for a year on selling Al Simmons to the Tigers after his slumping 1935 season. By keeping Simmons—whom they received nothing but cash for—the Sox would have strengthened their lineup in the best year the team had in a 25-season period.

title since 1917. But no matter how he rearranged his chess pieces, he couldn't do it. Before a mid-1940s slump that ended Dykes's tenure as manager, the White Sox regularly won more than they lost, but never finished higher than third.

There was some notable activity on Dykes's watch, however. On August 14, 1939, the White Sox played the first night game under the lights at Comiskey Park. Charles Comiskey II, son of Lou Comiskey, and eventually the younger generation relative who would fight hardest to keep the club in the family, flicked the switch. Charles II, who was just 14 at the time, had a better manner with sportswriters than many players, joking, "I think I'll hold out for $10 before I turn 'em."

Players like pitcher Thornton Lee, who won 22 games in 1941; Rip Radcliff, who hit .325 or higher three times in the late 1930s; and Taffy Wright, who hit between .322 and .337 four times, were some of the players who had their moments under Dykes. But not enough guys put together enough special moments at the same time to lift the team to a single pennant.

After Ted Lyons replaced Dykes as White Sox manager for the 1947 season, Dykes spent the next two decades managing in the minors and coaching and managing in the majors. He was involved in one of the most bizarre managing incidents in major league history. In 1960, while managing the Detroit Tigers, Dykes was traded to Cleveland for Indians manager Joe Gordon. It is the only managerial swap in baseball history.

Before his death at age 79, Dykes said his favorite team of the six he managed in the majors was the White Sox.

"The White Sox were the best club I ever worked for," Dykes said.

Wherever he managed, however, Dykes kept up repartee with those close umpiring friends. Once he was compelled to visit an ump when one of his hitters disliked a call. Dykes said his hitter thought the ball was a foot outside, not a strike, and just to be safe Dykes said he divided by six and still came up with two inches outside. That was worthy of protest, so he sauntered out to home plate.

"Did you call that wild pitch a strike?" Dykes asked the plate umpire.

"Let's go, batter up!" the umpire said.

"Maybe that pitcher saw you bury the body," Dykes replied.

"Batter up!" answered the focused umpire.

"I know blind people who make an honest living," Dykes said.

"Come on, batter up," the repetitious umpire said.

"Maybe you'll play on our team tomorrow," Dykes said.

"You're delaying the game, Dykes," the ump said. "Back on the bench."

"Any place you're not looks good to me," Dykes said.

"Okay, Dykes, you're out of the game," Mr. Umpire decreed.

"See what a strain it is to have some of your best friends umpires?" Dykes said.

By the NUMBERS **725**—The highest number of total plate appearances by any White Sox player in a single season by infielder Lu Blue in 1931.

Old Aches and Pains

It was mid-summer 1990, and the white-haired man sat with a companion at a table in the Home Plate Restaurant in Cooperstown, New York, at lunch time.

"That's somebody," a guy sitting at another table whispered. "He looks familiar."

A boy, perhaps eight, was sent over to the older man from a third table and held out a gleaming, unused baseball to ask for an autograph. He was shy and did not say much, but the man reached over and scrawled his name. The star of the show was Luke Appling, the Hall of Famer who was the firmament in the White Sox lineup from 1930 to 1950, the shortstop who was the anchor in the infield, a nonstop headline of good news at a time when most of the tidings were bad.

Appling was a contact hitter, and Appling's managers could pretty much mark Appling down for a .300-plus season every year. When Appling strode to the plate at Comiskey Park, the home-team fans chanted "Luuuuke! Luuuke!" It was praise born of years of appreciation watching a maestro with the stick.

Appling had incredible patience at the plate. There was nothing a pitcher could do to rattle him, make him rush, or heedlessly chase an offering not of his choosing. He gave pitchers a workout waiting them out. He fouled off pitch after pitch until he exasperated the hurler.

"He has worn out many a pitcher that way," said Ted Lyons, a long-time White Sox teammate of Appling's.

Appling once fouled off 14 tosses from Yankees pitcher Red Ruffing.

*Luke Appling poses
before a game in
July 1940.*

It is some strange talent to be able to knock foul balls almost at will. Handy, but it doesn't show up in the box score. Once, Appling hit a foul ball that hit the facing of the stadium's upper deck, bounced back, and conked a seat-holder in the head. A nearby peanut vendor guffawed over the incident, and Appling saw the reaction from the batter's box. He had not meant to hurt anyone, and the scene made him grouchy.

Appling told the umpire and opposing catcher to watch and said, "I'll fix him." On the next pitch, Appling swung, hit the ball foul to the same neighborhood, and bonked the peanut vendor in the head. Nice? No. Justice? Yeah.

TOP 10

Most White Sox Career Hits

	Player	No. of Career Hits
1.	Luke Appling	2,749
2.	Nellie Fox	2,470
3.	Frank Thomas	2,136
4.	Eddie Collins	2,007
5.	Harold Baines	1,773
6.	Ozzie Guillen	1,608
7.	Luis Aparicio	1,576
8.	Minnie Minoso	1,523
9.	Ray Schalk	1,345
10.	Buck Weaver	1,308

In the modern game, when managers grow fidgety as their pitchers exceed 100 pitches, Appling would be murder. Not that he wasn't a pesky killer in his time. Appling was the apple of the White Sox fans' eye while finishing 16 seasons over .300, batting .310 lifetime, and winning two batting titles. He also scored 1,319 runs and drove in 1,116.

Born Lucious Benjamin in North Carolina, Appling acquired his nickname of "Old Aches and Pains" from the variety of ailments he endured, or said he did. Yet Appling played in 2,422 games. He was a very active hypochondriac.

Although it was not as mysterious as the true age of Satchel Paige, there appeared to be some paperwork shuffling going on with Appling's birth certificate during his playing days. It was commonly reported that he was born on April 2, 1909, and late in his career, as age became an issue, Appling did little to clear up any discrepency. In a magazine story dated April 1950—the beginning of his final active season—Appling proved a big tease.

"Some people think 39 is pretty old for a ballplayer," he said. "But I like the age of 39. That's why I've been celebrating my 39th birthday anniversary for the last three or four years and expect to keep it up."

Maybe it was Appling's allegiance to the age that convinced comedian Jack Benny—who grew up north of Chicago—to stay 39 forever, too. Later, the *Baseball Encyclopedia*, the bible of the sport, adopted April 2, 1907, as Appling's official birth date.

Originally, Appling planned to obtain a college degree at Oglethorpe University in Atlanta. But after some experience in the classroom, he signed with the Atlanta Crackers of the Southern Association. Word reached him that the major league White Sox wanted him, and he took the train to Chicago, a cheap suitcase under his arm. After some initial misgivings and some very shaky fielding, Appling stuck around for two decades. It was reported that after Appling's initial workout on the Comiskey infield, he complained that the stadium must have been built on a junkyard. Those who knew the history recalled that the land at 35th and Shields had been rescued from existence as a dump by Charles Comiskey.

Unlike many shortstops of the first half of the 20th century, Appling was not a good-field, no-hit dandy. He was a good hitter and just a so-so fielder for several years. Taking ground balls until his hands blistered transformed his skill. The batting season Appling enjoyed in 1936, as the White Sox made a semi-run at first place for the first time since 1920, was the best in White Sox history. He batted a team-record .388 and established a team-record 27-game hitting streak.

Appling spent as much time on the bench as in the field during his first few seasons with the White Sox and split time at second base and third, as well. When Jimmy Dykes became manager in 1934, he turned Appling loose, coached him hard, and the player later gave Dykes credit for making him a star.

Once after Appling made yet another error in a game against the St. Louis Browns and walked off the field in gloom, Dykes, still the third baseman as well as manager, was next to him.

"Why do they always have to hit the ball to me in a spot like that?" Appling lamented.

Dykes was incensed and grabbed Appling by the arm.

"Don't you ever let me hear you say a thing like that again," Dykes roared. "You won't be a ballplayer until you want them to hit the ball to you in a spot like that."

DID YOU KNOW . . .
That left fielder Pat Seerey produced a still-standing major league record–tying four home runs in one game for the White Sox against the Philadelphia Athletics on July 18, 1948? Seerey, a seven-year major leaguer, played just 99 games for the Sox in 1948 and 1949, and was a .224 lifetime hitter. He produced the game of his life with home runs in the fourth, fifth, sixth, and eleventh innings. The last shot was the game-winner, giving the Sox a 12–11 victory.

Although Appling led the league in errors five times (on the plus side, also seven times in assists), he got the message and became a go-to guy in the field, as well as at bat.

When he was younger, the 5'10", 180-pound Appling was a football player, so he was no fragile daisy. But listening to him moan about all the parts of his body that hurt made him the object of teammates' ridicule. That's how he got the Old Aches and Pains nickname. Dykes was one who shook his head over all of Appling's alleged physical woes.

"If he had all of the things wrong with him that he complains about, he wouldn't have lasted two years," Dykes said. "He's built like a rock, you know, and I don't think there's ever been anything wrong with him. But to hear him tell it, he's never been right. He has a bad leg or a sore arm or a pain in the neck, or something he ate didn't agree with him."

Whatever the degree of danger Appling was in, without imminent medical assistance he survived well enough to keep on playing for the White Sox. He became a team institution and twice, in 1949 and 1969, when milestone votes were taken, Appling was selected the best White Sox player in history.

Asked to reminisce, Appling picked the August 5, 1933, game against the St. Louis Blues as the best effort of his career. On an extremely hot day, Appling collected five hits—three doubles and two singles—and said he should have had a sixth.

Appling participated in the 1943 game when the White Sox scored a team-record 13 runs in an inning. The explosion came against the Washington Senators on September 26. The team struck 10 hits in the inning, and Thurman Tucker (the lead runner who scored), Guy Curtright, and Appling pulled off a stunning triple steal.

Once in a while, such as when he broke a leg in 1938, Appling's injury worries were genuine. When he went into the army and missed one-and-a-half seasons during World War II, he considered retiring because he didn't know if his body would bounce back. But it did. From the standpoint of great players, Appling was the best White Sox contributor during his 20 years with the club. From the standpoint of being part of a great White Sox team, Appling lost out. He played at precisely the wrong time, the worst long-term drought in franchise history.

Stories about Appling's aches and pains went on and on. Did you hear the one about the time Appling limped into the batter's box, complaining of a sore leg and double vision, only to smack a hit? Did you hear the one about the time he told manager Ted Lyons he could barely drag one foot behind the other and might make it through an inning? Played all nine and stroked three hits. Or how about the time Appling told Jimmy Dykes the pains were so intense in his stomach he thought he had appendicitis? Dykes had a doctor look Appling over, only to find that his belly was fine, but that he really had a sprained wrist.

TRIVIA

What was the White Sox's highest team finish during the decade of the 1940s and when?

Answers to the trivia questions are on page 173.

"You have the most imaginative hypochondriac in the big leagues," the doctor told Dykes.

In 1964, after a healthy wait, Appling was voted into the Baseball Hall of Fame. The decision thrilled him.

"This makes up for my never playing in a World Series," Appling said. "This is the greatest thing that ever happened to me."

In 1970 Appling returned to the White Sox as a coach, but only stayed through 1971. He then coached for the Atlanta Braves. From the South Side back to the South. He remained a hitting instructor until his death in 1991. Less than a year after his cameo autograph appearance at the restaurant in Cooperstown, Appling died at age 83. An aneurysm of the aorta felled him and he passed away in surgery. Of all the aches and pains Appling spoke of during his career—and later as he aged—that was one ailment that eluded his thoughts.

A New Start

He pitched bigger than his size and he outlasted so many of the flame throwers who impressed scouts with their supersonic speed. The favorite southpaw of the South Side, Billy Pierce was businesslike on and off the mound, in uniform and out, and he still speaks the way he pitched, thoughtfully.

Pierce stood just 5'10" and weighed 160 pounds when his uniform was weighted down with sweat. Originally from Detroit, Pierce made a few cameo appearances with his hometown Tigers, but was traded to the White Sox for the 1949 season. The White Sox were in a three-decade slump, down so long they couldn't see blue sky without a telescope, such an American League afterthought that they frequently made the St. Louis Browns look like Yankees equals.

No player who signed on with the '49 White Sox was likely to buy management promises that things would turn around soon. There was no supporting proof. Going to the White Sox in those days was like being assigned to a military base in Siberia. But the long-awaited turnaround finally happened. The installation of savvy Paul Richards as manager, the dizzying wheeling and dealing of general manager Frank Lane, and an influx of young talent meshed, and in 1951 the White Sox finished 81–73, in what seemed to be the team's best season since Hannibal crossed the mountains riding on elephants.

Eddie Robinson, Minnie Minoso, Nellie Fox, and Chico Carrasquel were just some of the new faces. Pierce finished 15–14 and felt the atmospheric conditions changing around him.

"In 1951 it was a complete change from the team I joined in 1949," said Pierce, who turned 79 in 2006 and still lives in the Chicago area. "The fans in Chicago really took us to heart. With the fans, there was pent-up emotion."

Almost unbelievably for the fans and players who had been around, the White Sox became perennial pennant contenders in the 1950s. They were no longer stuck in the basement, but most seasons were the scrappy dogs nipping at the imperial Yankees' heels.

Pierce was a big reason. By the middle of the decade, he was one of the best left-handers in the American League. En route to a career record of 211–169, Pierce won 18 games in 1953, 20 in 1956, and 20 in 1957. He recorded an earned-run average of 1.97 in 1955, and at various times led the league in wins, ERA, strikeouts, and complete games, and three times started the All-Star Game. In 1958 Pierce carried a perfect game against the Washington Senators into the

Ed Walsh, 73-year-old former White Sox pitcher (left), compares pitching grips with hurler Billy Pierce at Comiskey Park as an all-star team of White Sox old-timers gathered to play an exhibition game prior to the White Sox–Baltimore Orioles game on August 10, 1954.

TOP 10

White Sox Innings Pitched

	Pitcher	No. of Innings Pitched
1.	Ted Lyons	4,161
2.	Red Faber	4,086⅔
3.	Ed Walsh	2,946⅓
4.	Billy Pierce	2,931
5.	Wilbur Wood	2,524⅓
6.	Doc White	2,498⅓
7.	Ed Cicotte	2,322⅓
8.	Joel Horlen	1,918
9.	Jim Scott	1,892
10.	Thornton Lee	1,888

ninth inning. He got the first two men out, but surrendered a double to pinch-hitter Ed Fitz Gerald.

The White Sox of the 1950s were fun teams to play on, Pierce said. There was a lot of camaraderie, and the club played exciting ball. For the most part, the team succeeded by being crisp with fundamentals, fielding well, stealing bases, and bunting for base hits.

"Everybody got along with everybody," Pierce said. "We had great speed. We had 3–2 victories, 4–2 victories. You don't win them all by luck."

When the resurgent White Sox of the mid-2000s revived the song, "Go-Go White Sox," it harkened back to the 1950s when on-the-basepath speed was a bigger rage in the city than on-the-road speed was with the fanciest sports car. Luis Aparicio came along and led the league in stolen bases every year. Minoso was a daring threat every time he got on. Jim Landis and Jim Busby could run. Pierce said the initial tone was set by Minoso.

Saturino Orestes Arrieta Armas Minoso broke into the majors with the Cleveland Indians after spending a few seasons with the New York Cubans in the Negro Leagues. Minoso was born in Cuba and, as a black Cuban, faced the same obstacles to integration as

American blacks did before Jackie Robinson broke the color line in 1947 with the Brooklyn Dodgers. Minoso's challenges were compounded because his first language is Spanish.

In 1951 Minoso became the first black man to play for the White Sox, and a combination of circumstances have made the likeable Minnie an enduring institution for the South Side club even into his eighties. It didn't hurt any that Minoso hit a home run in his first at-bat for the Sox off Yankees pitcher Vic Raschi. Minoso was an outfielder who spent parts of 17 seasons in the majors with a lifetime batting average of .298. He was a pin cushion of sorts in the batter's box because pitchers hit him with thrown balls so often, but he was a sparkplug.

Friendly and outgoing, Minoso was partial to wearing fancy clothes and driving Cadillacs—and he still is today. The fans love Minoso, and he loves Chicago. He was a favorite of past owner Bill Veeck, who admired Minoso's skills and demeanor, and kept bringing him back to the team. One way Minoso is remembered is for his startling, late-in-life, publicity-grabbing batting turns, 15, 20 years, and longer after his normal retirement. Minoso loved being back in the limelight and the fans lapped up his age-against-the-odds at-bats.

The comings and goings made Minoso a five-decades ballplayer, but for much of the 1950s, and especially when the White Sox were first showing signs of rejuvenation, Minoso was a key man in the lineup. Before Aparicio joined the Sox, Minoso led the league in stolen bases three times. During the 1953 season, Minoso scored from first base on a wild pitch. He convinced opposing pitchers to guzzle nerve-settling medication.

Minoso had a difficult life growing up in Cuba. He was raised partially by siblings, in poverty, and when he began to make good money he did not hesitate to treat himself to some of the good life. But Minoso never lost sight of where his good fortune emanated from.

"In my life," he said, "there is only one thing. To play baseball."

Jerry Reinsdorf, the White Sox chief owner since 1981, assessed where Minoso ranks as an individual in franchise history.

"Of all the players who ever played for the White Sox, and there have been some great ones," Reinsdorf said, "Minnie Minoso is the closest thing to a Mr. White Sox as there has been."

One of the other new arrivals in 1950, who helped change the image of the Sox from a downtrodden team to an upbeat, on-the-way-to-somewhere group, was shortstop Chico Carrasquel, who replaced Luke Appling as a starter that year and held the spot until 1955.

Carrasquel was the first in a line of phenomenal Venezuelan shortstops who not only infiltrated the majors in numbers, but seemed to have a special pipeline to the White Sox. Aparicio followed him, and then along came Ozzie Guillen. Carrasquel made four All-Star teams for the Sox.

Carrasquel was signed by the Dodgers in 1948 and said he couldn't speak any English. He was so lonely because of the language barrier that he looked in the mirror and talked to himself. At one point, Carrasquel said he ate ham and eggs five times a day because that was all he could order.

But it was a lot easier to make himself understood on the field. The team recognized that Appling was nearing the end of his career and, at the least, insurance was needed at his position. White Sox spring training was like an open microphone comedy club tryout, come one, come all, let's see what you've got.

TRIVIA

How many times during the 1950s did diminutive second baseman Nellie Fox lead the White Sox in hitting?

Answers to the trivia questions are on page 173.

"Appling was to play every day," Carrasquel said. "And I was number seven. I tried hard, I made the ballclub, and they put me in the starting lineup."

That season Carrasquel appeared in 141 games; Appling got into 50 and retired at the end of the season.

No longer the dregs of the league, the White Sox began churning out winning records, and between 1952 and 1956, under Richards and then under old Cardinals shortstop Marty Marion, they finished third each year. In '54 the team won 94 games, and in 1955 it won 91 games. The Sox had not won 90 games in a season since 1920.

Another new face in the 1950s was outfielder Jim Rivera, a solid performer who currently lives in Indiana, but who had a nickname that implied he had come from Brazil or the Congo. Players called Rivera "Jungle Jim."

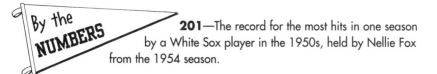

201—The record for the most hits in one season by a White Sox player in the 1950s, held by Nellie Fox from the 1954 season.

He acquired the appellation in the mid-'50s during a spring training game against the Dodgers in Vero Beach, Florida. He said a writer for the *Chicago Sun-Times* labeled him after Rivera ripped a Don Newcombe fastball for a single and then stole second base.

"I could hit a fastball," said Rivera, who spent more than eight years of his 10-year major league career with the White Sox. "I got into second base and I was swinging my arms back and forth. That's where the name came from. It don't bother me. It's better than some names they call you."

Management tinkered with the team, added new players, and still the Yankees, in the midst of the greatest run in American League history—10 pennants in 12 years—pulled away. Usually it was the Yankees. In 1954, when the Sox won 94, the Cleveland Indians set the then–American League record of 111 wins. The manager who upset the odds was Al Lopez, soon to make the transfer to the Windy City.

By the mid-1950s, there were solid White Sox players who never knew what it was like to have a losing season with the club. Gerry Staley, a stalwart relief pitcher, came over from the St. Louis Cardinals in 1957, where he won as many as 19 games as a starter. A careeer 134-game winner, Staley regularly appeared in 50 or more games a season out of the bullpen for the Sox.

Winning energized both players and fans, said Staley, who turned 86 during the summer of 2006 and is retired in Vancouver, Washington.

"It had been a long time since they had been winners," Staley said. "It put spirit in the people more. There's enthusiasm. A winning team means an awful lot. If you go to the park and you're losing, your spirit is already down."

As much as anyone else in the collection of good men with good attitudes and more skills than fans had been used to seeing at one time, a player who could instill spirit was second baseman Nellie Fox.

Fox was called baby-faced so often he could probably have done commercials for Johnson & Johnson. But the people who described

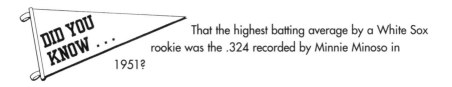

That the highest batting average by a White Sox rookie was the .324 recorded by Minnie Minoso in 1951?

him that way must have missed him smoking cigars. He stood just 5'9" and weighed about 150 pounds (meaning he probably never heard of steroids) and was described as "little" as often as a leprechaun. There was nothing little about the way Fox played, however. Fox played with big-time style and grit and a bulge of chewing tobacco that made his left cheek so fat it looked as if he were in the process of swallowing a baseball.

Fox, whose first name was really Jacob, was born in St. Thomas, Pennsylvania, in 1927 and broke into the majors with the Philadelphia Athletics in 1947. But he participated in most of his 2,367 games as a member of the White Sox. Fox hit .288 lifetime, made 12 All-Star teams, and was elected to the Hall of Fame in 1997. Unfortunately, that was well after his premature death at 47 from cancer.

Proficiency aside—and Fox was the best of his era at his position—teams need players who bring spark to the game. Fox was one of those guys who played hard all of the time and who could juice up those around him.

Casey Stengel, the Yankees field boss who was laughing all the way to all of those pennants with his jokes and his juggled lineups, said of Fox, "That little feller, he ain't so big, but he's all fire. He's caused me more grief than anyone else on the White Sox. He's in my hair all of the time."

Fox hunted and played Ping-Pong for off-season relaxation, and despite being hit by pitches and needing dental work because of erratically bouncing ground balls, he resisted ever being taken out of the lineup. One reason was his early major league experience sitting on the bench as regularly as a retiree feeding pigeons. What inserted Fox into the lineup to stay in the early 1950s was his hitting improvement. He jumped from .247 to .313 between 1950 and 1951.

"Until then, I'd come off the bench to fill in and then it would seem like I'd be back on the bench," Fox said.

In 1959 Fox received a surprising, unsolicited testimonial in the form of a handwritten letter from the aged Ty Cobb, perhaps the ultimate hardscrabble player and the one whom many call the best baseball player ever.

The letter began in low-key fashion: "As you know, I also played baseball..." Much of the rest of the letter detailed, after watching him play in the World Series against the Dodgers, just how highly Cobb thought of Fox's skills. "[T]o relate my admiration of your ability and play, fielding and at bat, your play is along the lines of the boys of yesteryear." Cobb praised Fox on many counts, including his talent at performing the hit-and-run, as well as being able to run and hit. "So Nellie it's refreshing to see a boy like you playing the real type of baseball.... I predict when you have to slow up, age, etc., that you are strictly managerial material. This is all, much luck and success."

A fairly impressive secret admirer.

Having guys like Fox and Aparicio anchoring the middle of the infield and strong defensive players at other positions was a bonus for a pitcher. Pierce appreciated how the slick fielders helped.

"Nellie and Louie saved us many, many runs," Pierce said. "Very rarely did a pop-up fall. They broke very, very quickly and they saved you runs."

That was the White Sox of the 1950s—they stole runs from other teams and scored just enough of their own to win.

Luis Aparicio

Luis Aparicio stood with his wife Sonia under the hot July sun behind the center-field stands at U.S. Cellular Field gazing at himself. The esteemed Hall of Fame shortstop from the 1950s and 1960s was positioned next to a symbol of the past that had brought him from home far away back to Chicago.

During those years, Aparicio and Nellie Fox were the best double-play combination in the majors. They served as the soul of the Go-Go White Sox, were All-Stars together, Gold Glove winners, and made for a formidable combo that defined infield defense in the American League.

Aparicio peered through wire rim glasses at a younger version of himself on July 23, 2006, just before the White Sox played a regular-season game against the Texas Rangers. A bronze statue of Fox shoveling the ball to Aparicio at second base was unveiled and the sculpture looked as real as old video.

"Way to go, Luis!" a fan yelled from the surrounding crowd.

Aparicio raised his fist in triumph.

"It's a great honor for me to be here today," Aparicio said in his remarks about the statue. "I would not rather be anywhere else today. Baseball is the best game. Thank you, God, for giving me the ability to play this game."

Indeed, Aparicio had great ability to play this game. Born in 1934, he grew up in Venezuela, was taught the sport by his uncle, Nestor Aparicio, and father, Luis Sr., and moved right into the White Sox starting lineup, fully formed in 1956 when he hit .266 and stole 21 bases. He was a slick glove man, knew the fundamentals, and ran the bases like a demon, leading the American League in steals nine

TOP 10

White Sox Career Base Stealing

	Player	Bases Stolen
1.	Eddie Collins	368
2.	Luis Aparicio	318
3.	Frank Isbell	250
4.	Lance Johnson	226
5.	Ray Durham	219
6.	Fielder Jones	206
7.	Shano Collins	192
8.	Luke Appling	179
9.	Johnny Mostil	177
10.	Ray Schalk	176

times. He followed one of his idols, Chico Carrasquel, as the Sox shortstop.

Carrasquel was established, an All-Star, but White Sox scouts thought so much of Aparicio that Chico was shipped to the Indians. It was a risk, but by Aparicio's second season, baseball men drooled when they mulled his fielding genius.

"He's positively the greatest I've ever handled," said White Sox manager Al Lopez.

During a White Sox–Yankees game, Phil Rizzuto, formerly a star shortstop for New York turned broadcaster, couldn't believe his eyes when Aparicio made a circus stop at short and blurted out, "No shortstop in the world can make that play—but Aparicio did!"

By their second year together, Fox was telling people that Aparicio covered so much territory with his glove that he was scooping up Fox's second-base-side grounders, too. A bit of an exaggeration, but a hint that Aparicio was no fielder who built his fielding percentage through failure to roam. Decades later, Aparicio remembers Fox sharing his knowledge of hitters and offering tips on playing the field.

"I learned a lot from him," Aparicio said, "about how to play this game, how important this game is for us."

During his 18-year major league career, Aparicio was chosen for the All-Star team 10 times and won nine Gold Gloves. He batted .262 and stole 506 bases. He accumulated that total when more emphasis was placed on the long ball.

Aparicio began his baseball career on the sandlots of Maracaibo, Venezuela, but was still a teenager when he started playing top-level ball for Gavilanes on a team owned by his father and uncle. He barely spoke English when the White Sox out-wrestled the Indians to obtain a signature on a contract and he was assigned to minor league Waterloo. Aparicio said he hired an English teacher pronto, so he knew how to order meals. He kept up his English lessons after that, too, including a stopover in Memphis when there was no other Spanish-speaking ballplayer with the club.

At 5'9" and 160 pounds, Aparicio, like his pal Fox, was small of stature, but renowned for desire. Sportswriters and headline writers insisted on referring to Luis as "Little Louie" repeatedly. It became an honorific, almost like "Senator." In admission both of his sports passion and his lack of size growing up, Aparicio once considered becoming a jockey. His dad told him to park those ambitions.

Aparicio made his living with his glove, but improved as a hitter, six times cracking .270 when many shortstops held regular jobs while batting in the .240s. Teammates Nellie Fox and Minnie Minoso offered advice. As he aged, fearful of losing his reflexes and bat speed, Aparicio worked harder.

"I worked at being quick with my hands," Aparicio said of spring training time investment in 1970. "I worked for hours with 'Iron Mike,' our batting machine in Sarasota. I practiced hitting balls back through the middle. After a little practice, I'd seldom miss. I figured every one of them would have been a base hit."

By the time he was in his thirties, Aparicio was a winter-ball manager in Venezuela and he seemed a logical candidate for a coaching and managing career in the United States Little Louie was the White Sox shortstop from 1956 through 1962, became a star all over again with the Baltimore Orioles, rejoined the Sox for three additional seasons in 1968, 1969, and 1970, then completed his career by playing three seasons with the Red Sox. When he retired, Aparicio had played 2,583 games at short, the most ever, and was elected to the Orioles

Sitting atop the dugout roof at Comiskey Park on September 29, 1959, Luis Aparicio is surrounded by a group of youngsters. The kids were admitted free to the park so they could get a glimpse of the American League champions, who were working out in preparation for the World Series.

Hall of Fame in 1982. During the height of his career, when every fan knew him, and he was rewarded with honors every season, Aparicio seemed to be on top of his game personally, as well.

"I'm a happy person," he said. "I get along with people. I think I dream about baseball every night. You can't get that baseball out of your mind. I try to, but I can't." He said he used to wake up abruptly if he made an error in his dreams.

Chicago fans were glad to have Aparicio back from the Orioles. To them, he was and always will be a White Sox man. The return deal was consummated at the winter meetings in 1967. When Sox general manager Ed Short called the player, Aparicio reacted strongly.

"Are you kidding?" Aparicio said. "Whoopee...that's the best news."

When Aparicio broke in, he looked like a schoolboy. When he matured, with darkish skin and dark hair, he resembled a model. Even as he aged into his seventies, Aparicio looked younger than his years. Aparicio, who had a career .972 fielding average at the toughest position, believed good reflexes paid off for him on the bases and on the field.

"I think you need three things to be a good shortstop," he said. "Good hands, quick reflexes, and smarts. And I think I had them all, so I guess I turned out to be a good shortstop."

TRIVIA

Which White Sox employee worked for the Chicago team and the St. Louis Cardinals simultaneously in 2006?

Answers to the trivia questions are on page 173.

Decades after the men were no longer teammates, former White Sox center fielder Jim Landis said he was frequently mesmerized by Aparicio's plays.

"I played behind him, and I'll tell you this," Landis said, "once in a while I got caught flat-footed watching a great play."

More than a decade after retirement, Aparicio was elected to the Baseball Hall of Fame in 1984 and delivered a moving speech.

"When I first came to this country 30 years ago, I was just a youngster with very little in my pockets, but full of dreams and a whole world to gain," Aparicio said. "There were moments of disappointments and

IF ONLY . . . The White Sox had not traded Minnie Minoso to the Cleveland Indians before the 1958 season, the team might have captured the pennant that season.

frustrations, but my love for this great game of baseball and the help and encouragement I got from my teammates and friends were stronger than the obstacles."

In Chicago for the statue unveiling, Aparicio mentioned that he visits the city four to six times a year. He usually keeps a low profile, but sometimes signs autographs and makes appearances.

"How can I forget those fans here?" Aparicio said.

Sonia, his wife for more than half a century, is a cousin of former White Sox outfielder Jim Rivera, and they rendezvous when Aparicio comes north. One thing Aparicio could not bring himself to do after retirement as an active player and while he was raising children, was leave Venezuela again for months at a time to manage or coach in the majors. So he has confined his managing to his home country.

Aparicio said he thinks all young Venezuelan boys want to grow up to be shortstops like Chico Carrasquel—as he did. Carrasquel did help make shortstops a more popular export than oil. The reality is that more kids probably look upon Aparicio for inspiration. Ozzie Guillen, the current White Sox manager and the team's shortstop from 1985 to 1997, is another in the line of All-Star Venezuelan shortstops. Guillen said he was a teenager when he met Aparicio.

"I grew up with his family," said Guillen, who talked with pride about the long line of Venezuelan shortstops from Carrasquel to Aparicio to Davey Concepcion and Omar Vizquel. "I think I'm the worst one. I'm at the bottom. We've always been lucky enough to have someone from Venezuela to play shortstop."

Guillen is loquacious, charming, a jokester who oozes personality. Aparicio is a reserved man. Guillen said Aparicio is a hero in Venezuela who would be more popular if he made himself more visible.

"If I was Aparicio, I might be president of Venezuela right now," said Guillen, who is the first Venezuelan major league manager. "I don't think our country loves and appreciates him the way he is here because he's a real quiet man. I think they should retire No. 11 [Aparicio's number] for good, in Little League, amateur, and professional baseball, so that it would be there in every ballpark you go to."

Such a declaration could be a fiat from Guillen if he became president of Venezuela. Asked if that was his next job, Guillen grinned. "Being president of Venezuela for one month, that's all I need." And what would he do? "Buy myself a bigger boat," said Guillen.

Aparicio was moved to see his old moves immortalized in bronze and said it was sad that Fox, who died from cancer in 1975, wasn't present.

"Nellie would have been happy today," Aparicio said. "We all miss him."

Guillen said he was pleased the White Sox did not wait longer to honor Aparicio for the same reason.

"It's a great honor for him to enjoy while he's still alive," Guillen said. "I always love it when people are still alive for these things. You can enjoy it and be proud of the moment."

Just before the White Sox began play against the Rangers, Aparicio was ushered to the mound to throw out a ceremonial first pitch. His throw to the plate was true. Unlike the usual routine when the first pitch is thrown by a local celebrity or sponsor, and a second-string catcher makes the catch, the man kneeling in a squat was Guillen.

Smiling after he nabbed the pitch, Guillen rose to his feet, and the men hugged.

Veeck—and as He Said—as in Wreck

It is appropriate that even 20 years after his death Bill Veeck is still making baseball fans smile. Each time a Chicago White Sox player hits a home run at U.S. Cellular Field, the colored pinwheels spin and the sky lights up with fireworks. Somewhere up above, the man who gave the world the exploding scoreboard is grinning widely.

Bill Veeck was a hustler (self-described), an entrepreneur, a forward-thinking, creative, fun-loving, baseball team owner who yucked it up with everyone from fans to sportswriters, and who for decades threw his heart (very large), and bank account (not large enough) into his passion of running major league baseball teams. It just so happened that two of those were the Chicago White Sox.

The bane of baseball conservatives and the best friend the baseball fan ever had, Veeck grew up in the game. His father, Bill Veeck Sr., was the president of the Chicago Cubs, and young Bill worked for the team as a youth, even after his dad's death. Veeck is the one responsible for installing the ivy at Wrigley Field.

He smoked, he drank, he laughed—he tried not to let health problems such as an amputated leg stemming from a World War II wound interfere—and not only did Veeck want to win baseball games, he wanted very much for home fans to have a good time in his ballpark. Veeck mingled with fans in the bleachers as he tapped cigarette ashes into the ashtray imbedded into his wooden leg, sent a midget up to bat, offered Ladies Day tickets, and myriad other promotions.

In the 1940s, baseball was definitely the national pastime, and owners operated with the ingrained belief that all that was necessary was to throw open the doors to the park and people would come.

Veeck wanted people to come who had never even thought of attending a ballgame. And he wanted every one of them who walked out the door to go home and tell their friends what a grand time they had.

"Baseball by itself is not enough," Veeck said. "It's got to be fun, even when the home club loses. It's got to be wrapped up like a Christmas package."

One game, Veeck allowed fans to manage from the stands while holding up signs to make calls. Once a fan named Joe Earley asked Veeck why well-known players were always being honored with special days instead of the average fan. So Veeck held a "Good Old Joe Earley Day" for that average fan. No promoter in baseball history has matched Veeck for audacity. In 1951, when he owned the futile

Bill Veeck, ever the showman, clowns around as he stands outside Comiskey Park holding the keys on December 16, 1975. Veeck was heard to say, "It's all mine."

St. Louis Browns, Veeck signed Eddie Gaedel to a one-day contract and sent the 3'7" midget to bat as a pinch-hitter. Naturally, the man with no strike zone to pitch to walked. Ten years before he died, Veeck said, "My epitaph is inescapable. It will read: 'He sent a midget up to bat.'"

Veeck owned the minor league Milwaukee franchise, then the Cleveland Indians and St. Louis Browns. He made enemies among the more staid American League owners, and his financial backing was always shaky. Somehow, Veeck campaigned his way back into the league time and again—twice with the White Sox.

Once, as he was watching the economic realities change before his eyes, Veeck said, "We will scheme, connive, and steal, and do everything possible to win a pennant—everything except pay big salaries." On another occasion, also giving a nod to unfortunate financial reality, Veeck said, "I don't mind the high price of stardom. I just don't like the high price of mediocrity."

TRIVIA

Once the White Sox turned around their fortunes in 1951, how many winning seasons did the team record in a row?

Answers to the trivia questions are on page 173.

Charles Comiskey's heirs kept the team in the family. Son J. Louis Comiskey ran the team until 1938, followed by his widow, Grace Comiskey, until 1956. Grace Comiskey became the first woman to be the chief executive officer of an American League team and the second to run a major league team after fighting off attempts by First National Bank of Chicago, trustee of her husband's estate, to sell the Sox.

Dorothy Comiskey Rigney, the couple's daughter, was the majority stockholder until 1959, with her brother Chuck the key minority stockholder. The club stayed in the founder's family for 58 years, and the field's name, Comiskey Park, stayed put throughout that period.

Under the terms of Grace Comiskey's will, Dorothy gained 54 percent of the team's stock and Chuck received 46 percent. By the time Veeck emerged as a candidate to buy the team, the siblings were engaged in a family feud bigger than any Richard Dawson ever presided over. In a series of court battles that stretched on for a few seasons worth of baseball, Chuck Comiskey tried to gain a ruling that at the least would force his sister to sell her stock to him rather than an outsider. It did not go that way.

When the case was being settled in March of 1959, Dorothy Rigney's attorney, Don Reuben, argued, "This is not Chuck Comiskey's stock. It is Mrs. Rigney's stock to have and to hold. She can sell it to whom she pleases, give it to charity, or destroy it."

Dorothy Rigney chose to sell the stock to Bill Veeck and his backers for about $2.7 million. And the marvelous first reign of Bill Veeck began. The White Sox in no way resembled the desperate St. Louis Browns Veeck had sold off on their way into transition into the Baltimore Orioles. The White Sox were coming off a second-place finish, had the respected Al Lopez in place as manager, featured stars like Luis Aparicio at shortstop and Nellie Fox at second base, solid players at other positions, and the indomitable Early Wynn at the core of the pitching staff.

Veeck bought a team that was ready to win and inherited a fan base hungry to fly a pennant over Comiskey Park for the first time since the soiled flag of 1919.

"I'm delighted to be back," said Veeck, who as a youngster sold soda pop at Wrigley Field for 5 cents a drink and his entire life disdained the wearing of neck ties. "My first goal is to stay out of court [Chuck Comiskey made sure he couldn't] and avoid any controversies. We'll save them for the Yankees."

Curly haired and redheaded, Veeck's first full-time baseball job paid him $15 a week from the Cubs' coffers. But he already knew what he wanted to do with his life. "By the time I was 12, I'd decided I was going to own a baseball team."

Humorously, Veeck's first wife was a circus equestrienne, and many accused Veeck of turning baseball into a circus during his ownership days. It was not a comment Veeck took as an insult, but rather a compliment to his promotional skills. Rather surprisingly, Veeck attributed his inspiration for the exploding scoreboard to a "rousing pinball finale," in author William Saroyan's story, "Time of Your Life."

Veeck was a showman who thought big, but was unable to run a deep pockets operation. What Veeck tried to do was make players feel wanted and appreciated. He might not be able to meet their

TOP 10

Last 10 White Sox Inside-the-Park Home Runs

	Player	Date of HR
1.	Joe Borchard	September 9, 2002
2.	Chris Singleton	September 29, 2000
3.	Paul Konerko	April 11, 2000
4.	Ron Karkovice	August 30, 1990
5.	Ivan Calderon	May 27, 1988
6.	Rudy Law	September 21, 1985
7.	Carlton Fisk	August 30, 1983
8.	Rudy Law	August 17, 1983
9.	Wayne Nordhagen	June 9, 1981
10.	Alan Bannister	July 23, 1977

demands for big-time raises, but he spontaneously rewarded them, acting like a big spender on a limited scale.

Right-handed pitcher Bob Shaw was the recipient of one of Veeck's bonuses after a good game. Veeck gave Shaw $50 and told him to go into Marshall Field's department store. "I want you to buy a $50 shirt," Shaw said Veeck told him. Only the conservative side of Shaw won out when he went shopping. "I bought five $10 shirts and it pissed him off," Shaw said recently while laughing.

Another time, Shaw, who spent parts of four seasons with the White Sox and went 18–6 in 1959, said he got a $300 gray, pin-striped suit courtesy of Veeck.

"If you did something special, he wanted you to have something special," Shaw said. "He was great. You know, I thought the scoreboard was great, too. I thought he was great for baseball."

Former center fielder Jim Landis, now living in California, remembers the generous paternalism of Veeck in the same way. He was a fans' owner, Landis said, and he liked to bestow gifts on players who produced.

"Once in a while he'd give you a $200 suit," Landis said, chuckling over the unexpected wardrobe changes. "He treated the fans good. After a while it got to be comical, with goofy things."

DID YOU KNOW . . . That after his first two seasons as manager of the White Sox, Ozzie Guillen had the same winning percentage—.562—as 1950s–60s manager Al Lopez, the last manager to lead the Sox to a pennant?

It can get very hot and humid in Chicago, and the White Sox played their share of afternoon games. To relieve patrons, Veeck installed a shower in the outfield seats. A withering fan could walk over, pull a chain, and cool off with a stream of water. It was not so different from little kids running through a lawn sprinkler for relief.

In the first installment of his autobiography, *Veeck—As in Wreck*, Veeck explained his thinking about selling and setting a tone when a new owner comes to town.

"Excitement is contagious," Veeck said. "It jumps from the fan to the non-fan and to a degree that is astonishing, it spills over onto the field and infects the players themselves. The first order of business when you take over a franchise that has been in the doldrums is to create the atmosphere that the new order has arrived, that we are living in historic times, that great things are in the air, and ultimate triumph inevitable."

That was not so difficult to do with a winning ballclub like the Sox, a team on the rise.

"It was a very exciting time," said pitcher Billy Pierce.

It was a team determined to interrupt the Yankees dynasty, to put its own stamp on the American League, and to end the four-decade pennant drought. Pierce said the club took its cues from players who were hard-nosed competitors. Perennial All-Star Nellie Fox was one of those guys who felt it necessary to crush any opponent in Monopoly, or any game.

"If you played gin rummy with Nellie and he lost one, you could hear him all over the hotel," Pierce said. "He'd give 1,000 percent all of the time."

The number one starter in the pitching rotation was Early Wynn, closing in on 300 victories. He was a pitcher regarded as mean by hitters, and the favorite quote attributed to Wynn was that he would knock down his mother if she crowded the plate. (Sometimes writers said grandmother.)

"There was no tougher competitor than Early Wynn," Pierce said. "He was a very, very tough competitor. It was old-time baseball." Pierce said he is not sure if Wynn ever really said he would brush back his mother or grandmother, but he believes it.

"He did knock down his son," Pierce said. "I was there."

If there was nostalgia about the end of the franchise's connection to the Comiskey family, no fan could complain that Veeck was either heedless of their needs or that he ruined the club.

When he led the Cleveland Indians to the World Series in 1954, manager Al Lopez was the only one to disrupt the Yankees' stranglehold on the American League pennant between 1949 and 1958. Now he was the boss of the White Sox.

Some would say the White Sox were overdue, as year after year they picked off third place or second place. One of the greatest seasons in White Sox history was anticipated for the entire decade. In 1951 the team set a franchise attendance record of 1.3 million. And if there was an omen that the 1950s would be better than the 1920s, 1930s, and 1940s, it could be read in a staged preseason publicity photograph that showed slugging outfielder Gus Zernial playing catcher and pitcher Joe Dobson playing batting coach for a star pupil—legendary actress Marilyn Monroe. Marilyn Monroe did not hang out with losers. Zernial and Dobson wore Sox uniforms. She wore short-shorts.

Go-Go White Sox, indeed.

By the NUMBERS — **8,000**—The White Sox won the 8,000th game in franchise history on August 1, 2003, by a 12–1 score over the Seattle Mariners. Ironically, the winning pitcher was Bartolo Colon, who did not stay with the team, and the losing pitcher was Freddy Garcia, who joined the White Sox in 2005.

The Summer of '59

"White Sox! White Sox! Go-Go White Sox! Let's Go-Go-Go White Sox, We're with you all the way!"

Those opening lyrics of the peppy White Sox song were never going to be as universally revered as tunes by Frank Sinatra or Elvis Presley. But the campy song became a hit for Captain Stubby and the Buccaneers as the 1959 Chicago White Sox chased their first pennant since 1919. The song was a hoot, a blast, and so was winning.

Children had grown up, had their own children, and begun to go gray since the Black Sox Scandal. Fans had lived with bad baseball, results that made them wince, and mediocrity for four decades. Since 1951, the Sox had hinted at better things. At last, the moment of truth was at hand. The White Sox of 1959 fielded a club that went down in team lore as one of the most special since Charles Comiskey's bunch had been a gleam in his eye.

"That was a great year for everybody," said pitcher Turk Lown, who now lives in Pueblo, Colorado. "We always had good ballclubs [in the '50s]. I didn't see why we couldn't have a really good team. There was a lot of optimism. That was a good team. It was like walking on a cloud."

The White Sox were coming off a second-place season in 1958. The Sox, their fans, many baseball people, were sick of Yankees domination. Could anyone please beat the Yankees? Sox manager Al Lopez, known as "El Señor," grew up in Tampa, Florida, and became an accomplished catcher in a long major league career. He was at the helm when the Cleveland Indians won a then-record 111 games in 1954. Now he was in Chicago, and he felt he had the horses again.

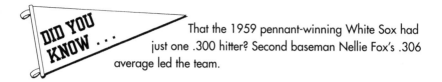

That the 1959 pennant-winning White Sox had just one .300 hitter? Second baseman Nellie Fox's .306 average led the team.

"The Yankees can be had this year," Lopez predicted at the start of the season.

Al Lopez was born in 1908 and broke into the majors with the Brooklyn Dodgers, playing a few games in 1928. He played 19 seasons and 1,950 games and was a wily catcher. He knew the game and proved himself an excellent managerial strategist. Above all, he wasn't scared of the Yankees. In 1957 ill-timed injuries and the lack of a bullpen closer prevented the Sox from breaking through. Lopez was voted Associated Press Manager of the Year, anyway.

Lopez wore thick-rimmed glasses, a determined look, and was patient with his players. He spied talent and developed it—notably center fielder Jim Landis—but he believed good baseball teams are built from the pitching mound out.

"I strongly believe the foundation of any ball team is pitching," Lopez said. "You get a few pitchers and you fill in around them. I don't mean nothing else is important, but pitching is the thing. Even if you've got a club that can score runs, pitching is at least 65 percent of the game."

Lopez was low-key in the dugout. He was a common-sense guy who sought to be a handler of men, not a prison warden.

"I try to manage them the way I wanted to be managed when I was playing," Lopez said near the end of the 1959 season. "They are adults making a good living and it's up to them to stay in line. If they don't and it impairs their ability, the best discipline I know is to get rid of them."

Lopez's philosophy was a good match for the 1959 White Sox. It was a mature team, with veterans setting a tone for younger players. The men got along well, socializing comfortably and bringing their game faces to the game. They were businesslike, devoted to their craft, and hungry to win a pennant.

Bob Shaw was in his first full year with the White Sox. Going on 26, he had only fleeting prior appearances in the majors, but turned into a big winner, going 18–6 to round out a staff anchored by soon-to-be 300-winner Early Wynn. Wynn was the ace of the staff in 1959, winner of 22 games and the Cy Young Award. In the majors since 1939, Wynn's public image was of a hard guy who was tenacious about winning, with a Mike Ditka kind of grit, someone who would wrestle a tiger for a piece of meat.

"He was all business—in a good way," said outfielder Landis.

Landis was an outstanding fielder with good instincts who roamed center field with confidence. Fielding brought him to the majors in 1957, and he batted only .212 that season, so Lopez told him to play winter ball in Venezuela. With his reputation as a good glove-man quickly established, and his deficiencies as a hitter on display, Landis knew his strength afield was keeping him in the lineup.

But one day he just flat out dropped a fly ball with Wynn pitching. After the game, when he saw Wynn approaching, Landis was quaking, prepared to be reamed out for his error.

TRIVIA

How many members of the 1959 American League champion White Sox were *Sporting News* postseason all-stars?

Answers to the trivia questions are on page 173.

Wynn walked up to Landis in the locker room and said, "Hurry up and get dressed." Landis said, "Yes, sir." Wynn said, "I'm taking you out to dinner." The older pitcher never scolded Landis for his mistake. Instead, he made Landis feel better.

The pitching staff included respected southpaw Billy Pierce, who won 14 games, Dick Donovan, Barry Latman, and the savvy bullpen duo of Gerry Staley and Turk Lown, who were road roommates, friends, and fearsome for foes to face.

"I was sort of a younger guy," Shaw said. "I learned a lot of things about pitching from them. There was nobody with a huge ego. It was kind of a regular-guy type thing."

Some people say team members don't have to love one another or hang out together to win, but it is definitely more fun when players are friendly. The White Sox of 1959 were more family than many teams, more buddies than strangers with numbers on their backs.

"If you wanted to go bowling, five fellas would want to go," Lown said. "If you wanted to have a beer, three or four guys would go."

TOP 10

All-Time Relief Wins for the White Sox

	Player	No. of Relief Wins
1.	Hoyt Wilhelm	41
2.	Wilbur Wood	32
3.	Gerry Staley	31
4.	Clint Brown	29
5.	Roberto Hernandez	28†
	Bob Locker	28†
	Bobby Thigpen	28†
8.	Red Faber	27
9.	Turk Lown	25
10.	Scott Radinsky	24

Landis, who lives in Northern California, said as a 25-year-old he revered veterans like the late Nellie Fox, Jim Rivera, and Billy Pierce, who protected him like a son.

"I still, to this day, when I see them call them 'my father,'" Landis said. "They took such good care of me. They were always bolstering me up. If I introduced them to someone I said, 'Here's my father.' That's how they treated me."

What Wynn provided, besides excellence, was a win-at-all-costs attitude.

"He was tough," Shaw said. "His outlook was that you're not going to give in to the hitter. He's always the enemy. He went 3-and-2 on every hitter, it seemed. He just battled. And every game would take three hours."

Lopez was right. The Yankees were ripe to be had in 1959. The White Sox had the necessary tools, finishing 94–60, five games ahead of Cleveland.

A critical four-game sweep of Cleveland at the end of August firmed up the White Sox's superiority, and although celebrating seemed premature, when the Sox returned to Chicago on August 30, an estimated 10,000 fans came out to cheer for them. It was a touch

IF ONLY . . . Local hero Ted Kluszewski had come to the White Sox in 1957 or 1958. The power hitter's addition might have driven the Sox to a pennant and established a mini-dynasty.

of insanity in a city that hadn't had an American League pennant winner since Woodrow Wilson was in the White House.

Lown, who turned 82 in 2006, said it was amazing to see the mob after the Cleveland series. "There was this fabulous amount of people waiting at the airport," he said.

Lown broke into the majors in 1951, won 55 games in his 11-year career, and joined the White Sox in 1958. Staley made his major league debut in 1947 and became a White Sox player in 1956. They were like brothers in the bullpen and were Lopez's secret weapon. The idea of a bullpen closer who pitched just one inning to finish off games with the lead had not yet been introduced in 1959. Lown and Staley were indeed rescuers, pitching several innings at a time.

Omar "Turk" Lown considered himself fortunate to pitch against the great hitters of his era in both leagues, from Willie Mays to Ted Williams. He spent most of his first eight years in the big leagues in the National League and caught Williams near the end of his career. Lown made the mistake of brushing Williams back with a pitch.

Third baseman Billy Goodman, a former AL batting champ and Williams's ex-teammate with the Red Sox, lectured him.

"What the hell are you knocking Williams down for?" Goodman said.

Too late.

"Before I got the ball back from the catcher, he [Williams] was back in the box," Lown said. "He never said a word. Then he hit one off the right-field wall."

In 1959 Lown went 9–2 while appearing in 60 games and garnering 15 saves. Staley led the league with 67 appearances, collected 14 saves, and had a record of 8–5.

"He was a good roommate," added Staley, recalling all of the hours shared with Lown in restaurants on road trips. Staley said their complimentary pitching strengths brought them both work.

"He had a little bit better fastball. I relied mostly on a good sinker to keep [hitters] off-balance."

No one could argue with the results.

"It turned out pretty good, didn't it?" said Staley, who was a starter before going to the bullpen. "Everyone seemed to have a pretty good year. The guys who didn't have that much experience had good years. It was a good feeling all over the city."

If the White Sox were short on one ingredient, it was power. In late August, owner Bill Veeck remedied the worry, acquiring first baseman Ted Kluszewski from the Pittsburgh Pirates. Big Klu was so muscular and so strong that he looked like the after picture on the back of a comic book ad encouraging 98-pound weaklings to bulk up. He cut off the short sleeves of his uniform to show off his bulging biceps and seemed like the last guy in the world you would want to tangle with in an arm-wrestling contest.

In 31 games with the Sox at the end of the season, Klu hit nearly .300 and became an instant fan favorite. Supporters began chanting, "Klu! Klu!" It didn't hurt any that he was a local, growing up the son of Polish immigrants in Argo, Illinois, a small suburb of Chicago, before playing football for Big Ten champion Indiana University. One of three boys, Klu said at 245 pounds he was the smallest. He said he had a sister who weighed 300 pounds.

Kluszewski said his father John was the strongest man in town and "would go to the kitchen table, bite it, and lift it right off the floor." That certainly said something about his jaw muscles being of alligator caliber. By the time he became a White Sox player, Klu had recorded National League home-run seasons of 47 and 49.

Within days of Klu's arrival, after demonstrating a Babe Ruth–type presence with vigorous, air-conditioning swings and misses and vicious line drives, Lopez said, "The first-base job is his. He reported here in a great frame of mind and he looks really good at the plate."

By the
NUMBERS

2.69—The team-leading earned-run average of Bob Shaw for the 1959 pennant-winning White Sox.

The acquisition of first baseman Ted Kluszewski from the Pirates late in the season helped push the White Sox to the 1959 pennant.

Big Klu hooked up with the Sox just before they completed the major sweep of the Indians and his 101 at-bats gave the team a new dimension. The White Sox rode their diversified attack, their pitching power, and their slick fielding to the league championship. When they clinched the pennant in Cleveland, they began partying immediately after the last out.

"Klu and I were together in the shower room and everyone was drinking champagne," said outfielder Rivera.

When the team returned home, the city went wild. Fans celebrated at the airport and in the streets. Billy Pierce said fans "rocked the bus a little bit." He said he grabbed a taxi cab with backup first baseman Earl Torgeson and watched with astonishment riding down main streets as people expressed their joy. Chicago was not exactly a city of pro sports winners at the time. Festive occasions did not come along as often as New Year's Eve.

"People in Chicago did it up real big," Rivera said. "Mayor Daley did it up real big."

Mayor Richard J. Daley, who had grown up a Sox fan, gave his approval to the city council to set off the city's air raid sirens in jubilation.

The siren was a distinctive way to welcome home the Sox. Only most of the city had no idea what was going on. It was the height of the cold war, and thousands of people alerted by the five-minute-long wailing associated it less with White Sox victory than with a Russian invasion. It scared the hell out of them.

But once the pennant party paused, fans sang their way to the World Series against the Los Angeles Dodgers: "Go-Go-Go White Sox!"

Early Wynn

Early Wynn's fastball turned American League batters into tap-dancers. Any swinger who dug in too deeply in the batter's box was likely to be eating dirt there. It was mandatory to be light on your feet because if this hurler thought you were crowding the plate, he was going to move you, none too politely.

Wynn was about as territorial as the velociraptor in *Jurassic Park*. Do not infringe on his turf or a fastball will be flying at your head at 90 miles per hour to brush you back. By the time Wynn came to the White Sox in 1958, his reputation was long-ingrained.

In 1959, when Wynn led the White Sox to their first pennant in 40 years, he was in the twilight of a major league career that had begun in 1939 with the Washington Senators. But he was the dominant starting pitcher in the league with a 22–10 record.

Teams win with a variety of weapons, but they always need good pitching. In the White Sox's case, they rode Wynn's broad shoulders throughout the regular season. He was a leader on the mound who was a no-nonsense thrower. Some of his teammates called Wynn "Grumpy," and they all knew that if they committed some sin to tick him off they would hear about it.

What Wynn's teammates always admired was the determination that propelled him to keep on fighting.

"He was tough," said White Sox outfielder Jim Rivera. "When he got out there on the mound, you'd better play good defense behind him or he'd let you know about it. What a competitor."

Solidifying his reputation as someone who despised all hitters, once Wynn attempted to plunk Hall of Fame third baseman George Kell while he was leading off from first base. Kell had

TOP 10

10 White Sox–Related Books

	Title	Author(s)
1.	Veeck—As in Wreck	Bill Veeck and Ed Linn
2.	Ron Kittle's Tales from the White Sox Dugout	Ron Kittle
3.	'59 Summer of the Sox	Bob Vanderberg
4.	Joe Jackson: A Biography	Kelly Boyer Sagert
5.	The White Sox Encyclopedia	Richard Lindberg
6.	White Sox: The Illustrated Story	Richard Whittingham
7.	White Sox Glory	Alan Ross
8.	Eight Men Out	Eliot Asinof
9.	Say It's So	Phil Rogers
10.	Sox and the City	Richard Roeper

driven five or six liners through the box during the season, and Wynn got fed up.

"I always considered that pitcher's mound as my place of business," Wynn said in 1962, "and I had no desire to see it cluttered up with blood, especially when it had a pretty good chance of being my blood."

Part Cherokee Indian, Early "Gus" Wynn was born on January 20, 1920, in Hartford, Alabama, and was only 16 when he signed with the Senators. During a 23-year career, he won 300 games and lost 244, but was a late bloomer who became a star with the Cleveland Indians after a trade in 1948. He won 20 games in a season five times, but each time a team decided he was too old and it was time to move on, Wynn proved management wrong. Wynn was a standout for the Indians under Al Lopez in the early 1950s, so Lopez knew what he was getting when Wynn joined the Sox. One game, when they were both with the Indians, Wynn did not have his best stuff and had surrendered five runs. Lopez made the trek to the mound to remove Wynn for a relief pitcher.

"I'm not coming out," Wynn said. "I can get this next guy." (Certainly a famous last sentence for pitchers.)

DID YOU KNOW . . . That in 1979, when former White Sox pitcher Early Wynn became a broadcaster for the Toronto Blue Jays, a 1977-minted expansion franchise, he had more victories on his résumé than the ballclub?

Lopez put his hand out for the ball, but Wynn took a few steps back and threw the ball into the manager's stomach. Ouch. Wynn was the type of pitcher who expected to be around for a long afternoon when it was his turn in the rotation. He recorded 290 complete games (and 49 shutouts).

"He could drive you nuts," Lopez said. "He'd get ahead two strikes, but then he tried to finesse the batter. He had a lot of 3–2 counts. It wasn't unusual for Early to throw 150 pitches in a game."

That's truly old school. If a manager left a starting pitcher in the game for 150 pitches these days, he would be vilified by fans and tarred and feathered by the media. But Wynn thrived on the workload.

Wynn nurtured his tough-guy persona on the mound. The legendary quote attributed to him about knocking his mother down if she was crowding the plate and a threat to win the game was exhibit A. Trying to get at the truth of the matter was like trying to get Satchel Paige to admit his age. Wynn enjoyed the gamesmanship.

"That was just sportswriter talk," Wynn said once. "But I might pitch her inside."

Wynn was indisputably the best pitcher in the AL during the 1959 season. He was 6' tall, weighed 220 pounds, threw fast, realized that his team was counting on him, and that it had a chance to do something special. That season he played even bigger than he was.

"I have four pitches," Wynn said. "My knuckleball breaks in any direction when it gets to home plate. My curve breaks down and away from a right-handed batter. My slider has a similar break, but it's a faster pitch, and the break is smaller and quicker. Then there's my fast ball and, of course, variations on all these pitches when I change speeds."

Wynn did everything but name the pitches. Wynn was all business, even if he had a droll way of discussing certain confrontations. Asked the best way to pitch to Red Sox Hall of Famer Ted Williams, the first thing Wynn said was, "Under cover of darkness."

Early Wynn unleashes another strike en route to a two-hit, 4–0 win over the Red Sox in Chicago.

Wynn's fierceness on the mound was shaped by a variety of sources. As a rookie with the Senators in 1939, Wynn said, manager Bucky Harris had a standing policy for pitchers.

"If you had two strikes on a batter and were ahead in the count, you had to knock him down with a pitch or you were fined $25," Wynn said.

Not wanting to throw away such a significant sum Wynn learned his lesson, and he carried it with him for the rest of his career. Why take chances? Twenty-five bucks was still real money in 1959.

Wynn was an equal opportunity fastball hurler with a single set of rules for all batters, regardless of stature. It was admirable consistency in approach, and he never wavered from it. Teammates said Wynn could be a nice guy off the field on days he was not scheduled to pitch, but he was so intense on pitching days that it was advisable to steer clear. No Wynn small talk in the locker room as he prepared for a game. Once the first pitch was thrown, Wynn wanted it known that he held the deed to ballpark property, that it was his game.

"He was serious about every pitch, every game," Indians pitching coach Mel Harder said. "He liked to have fun, but he was tough to get along with on the days he was pitching."

If more easygoing players or sportswriters could not fathom where Wynn's deep-rooted single-mindedness emanated from, he once summed it up for them.

"There aren't many jobs in the majors," he said. "Every hitter I face is a man trying to take money out of my pocket. Every hitter is an enemy. I can room with a man for five years, but if he comes to bat against me later for another team, he's not my friend."

Wynn's upbringing was a factor, too, in developing that football-player mentality. For one thing, he was a high school football player. Hartford, Alabama, was a small town and growing up there during the Depression meant that nickels were as prized as steaks. Hartford farms grew cotton and peanuts and a major league local wage was $15 to $20 a week. In his youth, Wynn said he traveled more by foot and horse and buggy than he did by automobile. It was easy to see why Wynn viewed every hitter as an "enemy" threatening to steal his lunch.

Wynn would not tolerate being shown up. It was part of cultivating an aura of intimidation.

By the NUMBERS

11—The number of times second baseman and future Hall of Famer Nellie Fox, a contact hitter, struck out during the entire 1958 season in 623 at-bats.

"Early had a theory that if you showed him up, you paid," said Billy Pierce, another pitcher on the 1959 White Sox. "But Early was very friendly off the field." Sportswriter John Kuenster said in his first year covering the team, Wynn took him to dinner. Relief pitcher Turk Lown called Wynn "a great man to know."

Neither Wynn, nor most baseball players, cultivated conditioning programs in the 1950s, but Lown has a vision in his mind of Wynn in 1959 putting himself through extra workouts. Lown said Wynn would don a rubber shirt to make him sweat more and dash to the outfield for some running.

"After he pitched, he'd come out and he ran and ran and ran," Lown said.

Following Wynn's superb 1959 campaign, his skills seemed to drop off quickly. He won 13 games the next season, finished 8–2 in 1961, and after going 7–15 in 1962, his career seemed over. There was one major problem: Wynn was stuck on 299 victories. Winning 300 games in the majors is a magic number. Wynn desperately wanted the chance to win that milestone game.

The 1962 season ended in disappointment for Wynn. He was 42, and in the closing days of September when he went after win number 300, he couldn't pull it off. He lost twice to the Yankees in the last 10 days of the season. Although there was much speculation that he would retire, Wynn would not say so.

Asked if he would return to chase the 300th triumph, Wynn said, "I don't know. I've got to think about it. I want it. I want it so bad. Maybe I'll come back."

Rather than keep Wynn aboard, and give him the chance he desired, in November the White Sox made Wynn a free agent, giving him permission to sign with any team for the $1 waiver price. Wynn returned to Cleveland, his old home, and appeared in 20 games during the 1963 season. He went after the 300th and finished the year 1–2. But the "1" was all that mattered. It came the hard way, on July

13, after giving up four runs to the Kansas City Athletics in five innings, but it was a day when his teammates scored seven runs.

Wynn retired at 43, making his home in Venice, Florida, where he had a boat and fished often. He was also a pilot and owned his own plane. Baseball had been very, very good to him. He noted that he did not have a high school diploma, but that the life experiences gained through baseball more than compensated.

"What with the people I've met, the places I've seen, and the things I've done, baseball has been both high school and college to me," Wynn said.

But Wynn was not through with baseball. Among other things, Wynn managed a minor league team in Indianapolis, became pitching coach for the Minnesota Twins, and served as a broadcaster for the Toronto Blue Jays. The most satisfying moment was Wynn's election into the Baseball Hall of Fame in 1972. The induction ceremony brought tears to the tough guy's eyes. His acceptance speech lasted only a few minutes.

TRIVIA

Which White Sox player said the following about the 1959 season: "The best thing of all is a winner for Chicago."

Answers to the trivia questions are on page 173.

"I don't know how come my hands are so wet and my throat so dry," Wynn said. "I don't believe the words are within me to express my gratitude for being elected into the Hall of Fame."

Wynn, who died of a stroke in April 1999 in Florida, spent a half century in baseball. There were occasional signs he was mellowing during his final years in the sport.

"I really wasn't as mean as people made me out to be," Wynn said.

Only when he had to be, when a pennant was on the line.

A World Series for the South Side

For one day, at least, it seemed as if a miracle of the past would repeat itself. When the Chicago White Sox defeated the favored Chicago Cubs in the World Series of 1906, the Sox were known as "the hitless wonders."

When the Chicago White Sox met the favored Los Angeles Dodgers in the World Series of 1959, the Sox were not exactly known as the "Bashing Batters." Pitching and defense made the Sox in '59. The Sox seemed to go out of their way to prove the point that hitting was not their specialty in a 20–6 April victory over the Kansas City A's. In the seventh inning, a *Ripley's Believe It or Not* inning, the White Sox scored 11 runs on only one hit, an almost impossible feat. Ten walks, one hit, a hit batsmen, and three errors contributed to the tally.

For all of that, when the first World Series game in 40 years was played at Comiskey Park on October 1, Chicago did claim an 11–0 victory, and the team actually earned some of those runs, though L.A. did contribute three errors in an inning that time, too.

"The pageantry was absolutely great," said Sox pitcher Billy Pierce, thinking back on the atmosphere in the Windy City.

The community went nuts when the Sox won the pennant. When the Sox crushed the Dodgers, fans were living out a fantasy come true. Could it be that the Sox would cruise to the World Series title?

"You know, for a while people said it was a fluke that we won because the Yankees had a bad year," said outfielder Jim Landis. "But the more I've thought about it over the years, we really did have a darned good ballclub."

Ted "Big Klu" Kluszewski paid dividends by demonstrating the meaning of his other nickname "Muscles" in swatting two home runs and driving in five runs in the opener before a crowd of more than 48,000 fans at Comiskey. Early Wynn got the win, with relief from Gerry Staley, but Kluszewski, then 35, was the man of the hour.

"It comes now when I thought everything was behind me," said a jubilant Klu of the late-career highlight.

Kluszewski hit his first homer off an inside slider and his second homer off a curve, and was surprised Dodger starter Roger Craig threw him off-speed stuff. A seven-run third inning left White Sox supporters giddy and the Dodgers needing four more throwers from their bullpen.

The big stage, and being thrust into the spotlight by his first-game deeds, shed new attention on Kluszewski's habit of trimming the jersey sleeves to flash his biceps.

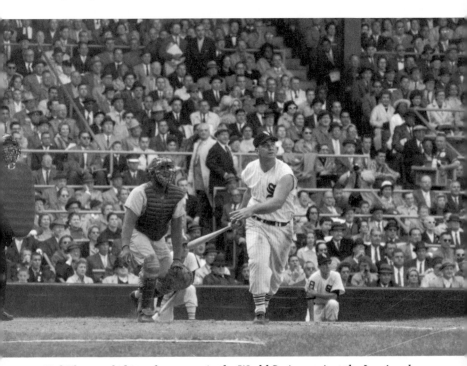

Ted Kluszewski hits a home run in the World Series against the Los Angeles Dodgers on October 1, 1959.

DID YOU KNOW . . . That the Dodgers attracted more than 92,000 fans to each of their three home games, a record unlikely to be broken because there are no ballparks in the majors with anywhere near that seating capacity now?

"Any uniform with sleeves binds you up here," Klu said, pointing to his shoulder. "It's cumbersome, so in 1947 I cut it off. Now I can't play with sleeves."

White Sox fans didn't care if Kluszewski went to bat in the nude if he kept hitting home runs. Alas, he did not keep up the same pace. Game 2 was also played in Chicago. Righty Bob Shaw was the Sox starter and he took a 2–1 lead into the seventh inning. The Dodgers' only run came on a solo home run by second baseman Charlie Neal. But then things turned sour. In almost every World Series, an unlikely hero emerges, a player who did not figure in the advance predictions, a bench player rising to the occasion for a moment of glory. One of those players in this World Series was Los Angeles outfielder Chuck Essegian, who struck a solo homer off Shaw to tie the game. Essegian, a former Stanford football player, was traded to L.A. from St. Louis during the season and had hit only one prior homer for the Dodgers.

Neal added a two-run shot for his second homer, and the Dodgers turned the game over to reliever Larry Sherry, who supplanted starter Johnny Podres. Sherry was another unexpected hero in the 4–3 win. Neal, who was only 5'10" and 160 pounds, did not compare to Klu in size, but like Hank Aaron, who did okay with his own wrist-hitting style, found other ways to bop home runs.

"Height and weight don't make any difference because it's your wrists that do the work," Neal said.

Game 2 produced one of the most famous and unlucky baseball photographs of all time. White Sox outfielder Al Smith was following the flight of Neal's first home run to left in the fifth and chased it to the wall. The shot did not land very deeply in the seats. As Smith looked up hopelessly, a cup of beer spilled and splashed down on his upturned face. It was adding insult to injury, and Smith was embarrassed and fairly angry. He thought a fan tossed the beer at him on purpose.

"I was ticked," Smith said. "But the umpire down the left-field line told me what happened, that a fan had lost it trying to catch the baseball."

The teams took a day off and resumed the competition at the Los Angeles Coliseum, a vast stadium of odd dimensions constructed primarily for football but used for Dodgers ball while Chavez Ravine was being built. Whether they were playing in the Roman Coliseum or the L.A. Coliseum, the Sox knew they had to take Game 3 to flip the Series around. But the Dodgers had gotten their sloppy game out of the way in the opener. Game 3 was the type of ballgame that make managers run for Grecian Formula to combat the gray in their hair and to consult accountants about their pensions. Call a séance and ask Al Lopez.

The White Sox cracked 12 hits in the game, three by second baseman Nellie Fox, two by shortstop Luis Aparicio, two by third baseman Billy Goodman, and two by catcher Sherm Lollar. Chicago pitchers held Dodgers batters to five hits. But the Sox lost 3–1 before a stunning 92,394 fans. The go-ahead run was produced by Dodgers pinch-hitter Carl Furillo's single up the middle with the bases loaded in the seventh inning. Future Hall of Famer Don Drysdale got the win, but Sherry slammed the door over the final two innings in relief once more.

Just to be back in the World Series was great for Chicago and for players who had waited whole careers for a chance to play for all the marbles. Relief pitcher Turk Lown said he runs into people who remember him being part of the Series team.

TRIVIA

What was the White Sox's team batting average during the 1959 season?

Answers to the trivia questions are on page 173.

"I think about it occasionally," he said. "People say to me, 'It must have been great.' It was great, ooh, definitely, but I wish our 1959 team accomplished what they did last year [in 2005]."

Suddenly, the dream was fading to black, the World Series title image etched in White Sox players' minds growing fuzzy. The Dodgers led two games to one and were still playing at home before the largest crowds in baseball history. It had been Early Wynn's year.

TOP 10

Top 10 White Sox Hitters in 1959 Series

	Player	Average
1.	Ted Kluszewski	.391
2.	Nellie Fox	.375
3.	Luis Aparicio	.308
4.	Bubba Phillips	.300
5.	Jim Landis	.292
6.	Al Smith	.250
7.	Billy Goodman	.231
8.	Sherm Lollar	.227
9.	Norm Cash	.000†
	Jim Rivera	.000†
	Jim McAnany	.000†

He was the staff ace, the stopper, and Lopez gave the hard thrower the ball with an implicit instruction—stop the bleeding.

"I went into the World Series last fall without a real book on the Los Angeles Dodgers," Wynn said in 1960. "The White Sox gave us long, detailed scouting reports on the Dodgers hitters, but it seemed like an awful lot to memorize in a short time. Those reports often give you more detail than you can use. It can get confusing. Actually, the main thing you want to know about each man is whether he is a low-ball hitter or a high-ball hitter."

Wynn did not have it for this critical game in front of 92,650 fans. He lasted just 2⅔ innings and surrendered four runs. Lown, Billy Pierce, and Gerry Staley each took a turn, and the Sox were still in the running at 4–4 in the eighth when Dodgers first baseman Gil Hodges slugged a homer off Staley. Dodgers won, 5–4.

It was Craig versus Wynn for the second time, but although he lasted longer, Craig did not figure into the final results. Once again, it was Larry Sherry in relief for two innings of no-hit ball. Sherry, born with a club foot that inhibited his participation in sports as a youth and forced him to run with a limp, was only 24. He was 0–0 as a rookie in 1958 but had emerged as a go-to guy with a 7–2 record

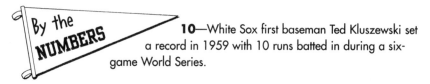

10—White Sox first baseman Ted Kluszewski set a record in 1959 with 10 runs batted in during a six-game World Series.

and three saves during the 1959 regular season. His brother, Norm, was a catcher with the Dodgers, but appeared in only two regular-season games.

It seemed that every time the White Sox threatened during the game (and they did with 10 hits, including three by Fox) and the Series, Sherry was like a traffic cop raising his hand and causing the approaching automobile to screech to a halt. He had that kind of effect on the White Sox offense. He was even bigger than Essegian. The Dodgers were managed by Hall of Famer Walter Alston, and although tempted to start Sherry, the pitcher had made himself too valuable out of the bullpen.

"I'd like to start him," Alston said. "But I can't afford to. If I start him, it means I can't use him in relief. By leaving him in the bullpen, I can get two games out of him for every one he would start."

How could the Sox stay alive? Down 3–1 in the Series, their prognosis was much like a patient delivered a terminal diagnosis and pinning his hope on a miracle drug rushed to the market.

To stay in business, the White Sox only had to beat future Hall of Famer Sandy Koufax. Koufax was about to embark on possibly the greatest five-year stretch of any pitcher in history. He gave up one run, and that was a very precious run for the Sox. Nellie Fox started the "rally" with a single to right field, advanced to third on a Jim Landis single, then scored as Sherm Lollar hit into a double play. Sexy? No. Effective? Yes.

Despite accumulating nine hits in 7⅓ innings, the Dodgers could not rattle Bob Shaw. But he departed with the bases loaded in the eighth in favor of Dick Donovan. Donovan pulled a Larry Sherry and gave L.A. nothing over the final two innings. Down 3–2 in games, the Sox still had a pulse.

In the locker room, Early Wynn shouted, "We're glad we're taking the Dodgers back to a legitimate ballpark!"

Wynn was right that a return to Chicago and Comiskey Park was something to cheer about. If they had it in them to make a charge, the odds were better that it would happen on the shore of Lake Michigan rather than on the shore of the Pacific Ocean.

Neal had not been complimentary about his American League adversary, suggesting the White Sox would have placed no better than fourth in the National League. Lopez chose to give the start to his hardiest competitor, Wynn, on two days' rest, and the fastballer was well versed in Neal's comments.

"We intend to make them eat their words," Wynn said.

It did not play out that way. The Dodgers scored two runs in the third inning and six in the sixth en route to a 9–3 win. All of Chicago's runs came on a fourth-inning homer by Ted Kluszewski. The Sox were still on the radar screen when Alston relieved Johnny Podres with his new main man—Sherry. And that was it. Sherry, who won two games and saved the other two Dodgers victories, was untouchable for 5⅔ innings. The White Sox dream died on their own field, and when the game was over, the Dodgers were both toasting and drinking Sherry in celebration.

"In the first game, when we won 11–0, everything we did went right," Pierce said. "And then for some reason our hitting wasn't there."

And neither was winning. The return to prominence was special, and the players and the city saw it as the beginning of a new era for White Sox baseball. They never imagined that another 46 years would pass before the Sox made it to the World Series again.

The Post-Series Blues

After winning one pennant, you come out of October thinking, "Why can't we do it again?" It is often said that repeating is the most difficult challenge in team sport, but after the 1959 World Series the White Sox looked themselves in the mirror and saw a team of Prince Charmings, a team that looked young and handsome and ready to take over the American League.

"We thought we could win again," said twirler Billy Pierce. "But then we traded away a lot of our young ballplayers."

He was right. Gone was future catcher Johnny Romano. Shipped away was first baseman Norm Cash, a future batting champ. Exiled from Chicago was pitcher Barry Latman. The Sox waved good-bye to catcher Earl Battey and outfielder Johnny Callison, future All-Stars.

There was no new dynasty, only thoughts about what might have been. And as much as they liked him, players blamed owner Bill Veeck for too much tinkering.

"*His* team didn't win the pennant," Pierce said. Veeck inherited the bunch that made good in '59, and he wanted to put his own stamp on the club. The maneuvers didn't work.

With a snap of the fingers, the magic was gone. Early Wynn turned ordinary, showing his age after the brilliant 1959 season. He finished 13–12. The White Sox needed to mix young players into the group, to add bench strength, and Veeck's trades cost them.

"They broke up the ballclub the very next year," said outfielder Jim Landis. "He took out the heart of the ballclub."

The White Sox finished 87–67, good enough only for third place. With Al Lopez at the helm and the farm system still producing well,

Al Lopez, who would manage good but not great White Sox teams after the magical 1959 season, is shown during his playing days.

the White Sox did not fade out of contention. They produced great moments, but could not put together a run like 1959.

One newcomer to the pitching staff was Joel Horlen, who came up for a cup of coffee in 1961 and stayed in the majors for 12 years while winning 116 games. On September 10, 1967, nearing the end of his greatest season in the majors, Horlen pitched a no-hitter against the Detroit Tigers. Horlen, who finished 19–7 that season with a league-leading winning percentage of .731 and a league-leading earned-run average of 2.06, won the game 6–0 in the Sox's first no-hitter in a decade. A 6', 175-pound right-hander, Horlen was born in Texas and attended Oklahoma State, pitching in the College World Series. He was going on 70 years old when he reflected on that outing from his home in San Antonio.

The night before the game, Horlen went out to eat with third baseman Ken Boyer and they bumped into the Tigers' Norm Cash and Eddie Mathews, then at the end of his Hall of Fame career. In the spirit of baseball fondness, the twosomes bought each other a round of drinks. Then Horlen watched some television.

There was nothing unusual about Horlen's routine on the day of the no-hitter. During batting practice he walked around the outfield. Then he sat down and read. Horlen was throwing to catcher J.C. Martin that day, and it seemed as if Martin practically read his mind with his signals.

"I never shook him off," Horlen said. "My sinker was really good that day. There were lots of ground balls. I never thought I'd ever pitch a no-hitter."

It is baseball superstition for teammates to ignore a pitcher in the dugout when a no-hitter is underway, but Horlen said he realized he was throwing one of those cherished games in the sixth inning. It just might be that Horlen was an unlikely candidate for nerves because of something that occurred in the game to distract him.

"I didn't feel anything was different that day," Horlen said. "Except that the team got five runs in the first inning. The big thing I remember in that game is that I hit [Tigers catcher] Bill Freehan high up on the left arm with a pitch."

Tommy John and Gary Peters were also members of the Sox rotation at the time and had both already hit Freehan with pitches in

By the NUMBERS

10—After posting 17 straight winning seasons, the White Sox finished 67–95 during the 1968 season. The slide was not gradual. The Sox lost a franchise-record 10 straight games to begin the season.

the same spot on his body. After he plunked Freehan, Horlen, who was friendly with Freehan and had played golf with him, yelled, "Are you all right, Bill?" Freehan replied with a string of expletives.

Horlen's expression of concern did not mollify the Tigers. They sought take-the-law-into-your-own-hands vengeance. Dave Wickersham was the Detroit pitcher when Horlen came up to bat. The first pitch was way inside.

"I go down in the dirt," Horlen said. "They let me know they didn't appreciate it [hitting Freehan]. The next one is at my waist. The next one is at my legs. It hit on the bone inside of my right knee. I went down in a heap. And I limped to first base."

The incident could have easily blown Horlen's concentration and cost him his no-hitter. But he held it together. Rather than sitting down on the dugout bench between innings, Horlen, worried his leg would stiffen and force him out of the game, chose to alternately pace back and forth in the dugout and back and forth in the clubhouse.

"I never sat down the rest of the game," Horlen said.

When the game ended, an ecstatic Chicago Mayor Richard J. Daley asked Horlen to pose for a picture with him. Horlen's biggest problem by then was standing still.

"Now my leg *is* starting to stiffen up," Horlen said. He made it through the photo op, however, and when Horlen peeled off his uniform in the locker room, his leg was black and blue from the point of contact down to his ankle. It was the color of the sky before a major rainstorm.

"It didn't look too pretty," Horlen said.

Although the bruise colors eventually faded, Horlen retained a souvenir from the no-hitter. He kept a game ball and preserved it in a little case in his Texas home.

One of the most memorable performers in White Sox history played a key role on the team from 1963 to 1968. It is unlikely that

DID YOU KNOW . . . That during their 98-victory season of 1964, the White Sox were never more than 4½ games out of first place the entire year and won their last nine regular season games, only to have the Yankees win 15 of their final 19 games to hold them off?

any pitcher befuddled more hitters—and catchers—with his stuff than knuckleball specialist Hoyt Wilhelm. Not only did batters get fooled by the ball's flight path, catchers couldn't catch it, either. Wilhelm was no phenom. He broke into the majors in 1952 and stuck around for 21 seasons, winning 143 games, saving 227, while appearing in 1,070. Wilhelm's career earned-run average was 2.52. His efforts eventually won him a plaque in the Baseball Hall of Fame. The five-time All-Star was the first reliever elected to the Hall in 1985.

To explain just how thoroughly Wilhelm was able to confuse batters, it is appropriate to listen to Pulitzer Prize–winning sports columnist Jim Murray, who described his knuckleball this way: "'The Moth,' the players call it. 'The Iron Butterfly.' 'The Dancer.' 'The Bat.' It comes up to the plate just faster than a postcard. It takes more detours than a small boy on his way home from school in spring."

The dipsy-doodle route of the ball to the plate drove everyone nuts. Wilhelm, who was still pitching in the majors during his 50th year on earth, had enough otherwordly stuff to provoke former White Sox manager Paul Richards to invent a newfangled catcher's mitt when both were with the Orioles. It seemed as large as a hub-cap, but it did make life easier for Wilhelm's catcher.

Wilhelm was a pioneer of relief pitching, the man managers used most often in short relief. The word "ageless" was used more often to describe him than "Mr." If Wilhelm stuck around much longer he would have been pitching to players young enough to be his grand-sons. That was appropriate, however, because Wilhelm, who won a Purple Heart at the Battle of the Bulge, did not break into the majors until he was turning 30.

"Really, I believe I'm as good now as I ever was," Wilhelm said in 1966. And in 1967, when he was asked how long he could continue, Wilhelm said, "Anybody who has taken a look at my pitching figures last season certainly can't seriously suggest I am washed up. I had the best earned-run average of my life [1.66]."

When Wilhelm died at age 80 in 2002—and, no, he wasn't still pitching in the majors up until the night before—his former Sox teammate Tommy McCraw praised his specialty pitch.

"He had the best damn knuckleball I've ever seen," McCraw said. "When he got a lead, he made it stand up. He made us a lot of money."

Not from extra World Series shares, however.

By 1967 the White Sox had turned over most of the roster from the pennant-winners. But, more significantly, the team had turned over ownership again. It was Bill Veeck's dream to run a ballclub in his hometown and he got his chance in 1959 when he took the reins from the Comiskey family. But Veeck was underfinanced and needed a constant winner and extra strong fan support to keep things rolling.

TRIVIA

What was lefty pitcher Gary Peters's earned-run average when he led the American League for the White Sox, and what two years did he accomplish the feat?

Answers to the trivia questions are on page 173.

And then there was his health. Ever since he lost part of one leg in World War II, Veeck suffered various illnesses and endured various operations. The physical woes grew more serious, and for a time it was debatable whether Veeck or his bank account would end up on the critical list. Veeck sold out to Arthur Allyn Jr. in 1961 for $2.9 million. It was a melancholy departure.

Veeck had introduced his share of innovations. The exploding scoreboard was his brainchild, and it remains in place today. Adding last names to the backs of uniforms in 1960 was his idea and remains a popular practice across the major leagues.

Fans were stunned when Veeck pulled out. They thought he was a long-haul guy, and the White Sox had won their first pennant in four decades on his watch. He was the fans' best friend, and the players appreciated his efforts, too. The one who expressed the sentiments most emphatically was old pitcher Early Wynn, who wrote an open letter to Veeck after the owner announced he was departing.

The letter read in part, "Dear Bill, I'm a better pitcher than I am a letter writer—at least I hope I am—but I'm writing now, not just for myself, but for all the other fellows who have played and worked for you on the White Sox. None of us want you to leave town without some sort of good-bye, or at the least a so-long, because we know you'll be up and kicking, bad leg and all, and that you'll be back with us soon."

That was a bit of foreshadowing no one could have foreseen.

"I know I speak for all of us," Wynn continued, "when I say that you've been a helluva lot more than just a boss. You've been a wonderful friend. All of us will always cherish your friendship."

Veeck's doctors prescribed rest—not his strong point. After the sale, Veeck packed his family into a station wagon emblazoned with "Chicago White Sox" on the side, and settled in Easton, Maryland. For a while.

The White Sox settled into...contendership? From 1951 through 1967, the Sox produced a winning season every year. But except for 1959, the Sox did not win a pennant. Not even in 1964; they won 98 games and placed second by one measly game.

Lopez always had the Sox on the cusp, but they could never quite take the last step.

The South Side Hit Men

Arnold Schwarzenegger made the phrase "I'll be back" a trademark in his action movies, but Bill Veeck beat him to it. When Veeck drove off into the sunset after selling the team in 1961, the only way baseball fans expected to see him back in Comiskey Park was as a spectator.

The odds were probably better that Frank Sinatra would perform the hula on State Street than Veeck becoming White Sox owner again. But Chicago was his kind of town. Some way, the man with the too-small bank account and the too-fragile health found love lovelier the second time around.

Veeck was older, perhaps wiser, but just as committed to putting on a good show when he returned in 1976 as he was when he left in 1961. And he burned for a winner again, even if the changing economics of the game, with free agency granted to the players, made it tougher to compete in the marketplace.

One thing Veeck was always good at was bringing excitement to the sport, to his team, and the ballpark. Veeck assumed the presidency for the second time carrying an index-card file of ideas accumulated during his 14-year absence from the sport. Perhaps the most important aspect of Veeck's second purchase was the rescue of the old-time franchise from being transferred to Seattle. Whether Veeck won or lost, at least he saved the team for Chicago.

Consistent with the showman's theory that the worst thing is public silence, Veeck made a bold move that got everyone talking about him and the White Sox. He announced that the 1976 White Sox would do something never before done in major league baseball history. The bottom half of their uniforms would be...short pants. Yes, shorts. Well, sometimes. Maybe.

Actually the fashion show began in April with the unveiling of a navy blue uniform with the tops hanging loose instead of being tucked into clam-digger pants. It was announced that shorts were optional. Veeck, aka Coco Chanel II, designed the outfits, with help from his wife Mary Frances, and said players would have greater freedom of movement.

"I haven't met a woman who has seen the uniforms who didn't want a blouse just like it," Veeck said.

Minnie Minoso, then a coach for the White Sox, models the memorable uniforms that the 1977 South Side Hit Men made famous.

At least he employed a manager with a sense of humor. Paul Richards was back in the dugout.

"He can go to Paris and be a sensation," Richards said.

Veeck didn't need to fly across an ocean to create a sensation. When he introduced the Bermuda shorts version of the unis, there was considerable response. Designed to be

TRIVIA

What was a popular rhyming banner hung at Comiskey Park to urge on slugging Richie Zisk during the 1977 South Side Hit Men season?

Answers to the trivia questions are on page 173.

cooler attire in the summer heat and humidity, Comiskey organist Nancy Faust provided a woman's review of the outfit. "Sexy, sexy," she said. "The ladies are going to love them."

The players did not. The shorts came out of the closet for the first game of a doubleheader against the Kansas City Royals in August. Not surprisingly, the Sox took some ribbing from their opponents.

"You guys are the sweetest team we've seen yet," said K.C. first baseman John Mayberry, who added in an aside to White Sox outfielder Ralph Garr, "You get over to first base and I'm going to give you a big kiss."

Despite having a wooden leg, Veeck was not shy about modeling the uniform, but others took abuse. White Sox pitcher Dave Hamilton said of reliever Clay Carroll, "He looks like a pilgrim going out to shoot wild turkey."

The lifespan of the shorts was short. And despite everyone's best efforts, the experiment was not easily forgotten. That may be because no other major league team has ever worn shorts again. Call it a swing and a miss.

Veeck returned at a propitious time. Attendance was poor and showmanship seemed like the right antidote to the mood of depression that not even selected stars could alleviate.

Third baseman Bill Melton swatted 33 home runs and drove in 96 in 1970 and led the league with 33 more homers in 1971. But the team was horrible in 1970 (56–106) and mediocre in 1971. The amazing thing, given that the home-run era had begun in the 1920s, was that no Sox player had ever before hit more than 29 in team history, so Melton's first season of 33 marked a team record.

IF ONLY . . . White Sox owner Bill Veeck could have retained big hitters like Richie Zisk and Oscar Gamble from the 1977 team, he could have built on the momentum of the South Side Hit Men's good will.

"It was the best kept secret in baseball," Melton said. "I knew I hit 33, but I don't think anybody else did. The worst thing in the world is to play for a last-place team because you can do no right."

There was a time when the Philadelphia Phillies and the baseball establishment felt that Richie Allen could do no right. The angry young man from Pennsylvania coal country was regarded as a troublemaker, at least partially because he felt strongly about racial issues, but also because he missed planes and was chronically late for events.

Better known as Dick following the 1972 signing of a $750,000, three-year contract that made him the highest paid player in baseball history at the time, Allen was far more popular as a first baseman in a White Sox uniform. In a classic photograph, Allen graced the cover of *Sports Illustrated* in a Sox outfit, a cigarette dangling from his lips, while juggling three baseballs. Allen led the American League in homers with 37 in 1972 and with 32 in 1974. He was named the league MVP in '72.

"I have found a home here in Chicago," Allen said. "It really has made me feel like a human being. Before, I was hidden, now I'm a little more outgoing."

Allen retired with two weeks remaining in the 1974 season, complaining of a bad back, but he came back and played for other teams through the 1977 season.

One reason the White Sox were able to obtain southpaw Jim Kaat during the 1973 season for the waiver-wire bargain price was a feeling in Minnesota that the pitcher, approaching his 35th birthday, was getting old. Kaat won 21 games for the White Sox in 1974 and 20 the next year. Kaat did not retire until 1983 after 25 years of major league pitching. He was still in the game in 2006, broadcasting for the New York Yankees before retiring after the season.

There is a suggestion with pitchers that as they age they slow down. In the mid-1970s Kaat altered his motion. He did away with his windup and began throwing quicker from the mound after the catcher tossed the ball back to him.

"Kitty Kaat," who won 283 games, went to what he called his "Joe Namath release." Quarterbacks do thrive on a quick release. Kaat did not change sports, however. He got hitters out until just shy of his 45th birthday.

Those great players never lived through the fan worship for the 1977 team. One player from that era devoted to Veeck's memory is third baseman Eric Soderholm. Soderholm was a regular with the Minnesota Twins until tearing up his knee. He was inactive the entire 1976 season.

"He was a great, great owner," Soderholm said recently of Veeck. "I loved the guy. He gave me a chance to play when Calvin Griffith gave up on me. He used to think, 'How can I make it interesting for the fans?' He was a carnival guy."

In 1977 Veeck's team played the big top. The squad of that season is one of the most beloved in White Sox history—the South Side Hit Men.

Expectations were low, but although weak on pitching depth, the Sox went nuclear. Forget bunts, the Sox embraced home runs. The Sox gave the fans pennant hope.

"We are one gigantic 'Rocky,'" said Richie Zisk, comparing the Sox to the underdog boxer Rocky Balboa in the public eye at the time. "Bill Veeck is a genius. Every move he makes is the right move. Everything he does comes up roses."

Veeck did not have the money bags to compete for stars with the game's wealthiest teams on long-term contracts. What he could do, and saw as his salvation, was sign players for one year. The rent-a-player strategy paid off with a 90–72 season and a club that contended for the West Division title.

"I think it was a bunch of guys who were castoffs from other teams, or guys like me who were injured and felt we had something to prove," said Soderholm, a nine-year major leaguer who hit .280 with 25 home runs for that team and won the American League Comeback Player of the Year award. "Bill Veeck put something together, and we were all able to jell. That magic word, 'chemistry,' was involved. Then we caught fire and we got momentum.

"We were scoring a lot of runs. We just started believing in ourselves and then we got the nickname, 'the South Side Hit Men.' I thought it was appropriate. I thought it fit." The Sox hit 192 that season. "It was just one of those magical years. I remember that year better than any other year."

Under manager Bob Lemon, the Sox were in a divisional race with the Royals and Twins and sat in first place from July 1 to August 12. The team acquired its own theme song, "Na Na Hey Hey (Kiss Him Goodbye)." Players like Richie Zisk, who was playing out his option when he signed with Chicago, said good-bye to a lot of baseballs. Zisk hit 30 home runs and drove in 101 runs. Oscar Gamble, possessor of a Jimi Hendrix–caliber Afro haircut, hit 31 home runs and drove in 83. Chet Lemon hit 19 home runs and drove in 67. The fans were boisterous, enthusiastic, and as willing to believe in the Sox as youngsters are in Santa Claus.

"It was a real nice ride," Soderholm said. "Nobody expected it. In Las Vegas we were probably 100-to-1 shots. We could be down 7–0 and you wouldn't see people leaving the park because they knew we had the capability of coming back."

Lemon can still hear the "Na Na Hey Hey" tune in his head. Spectators were so giddy that whenever the big guns blasted a home run, fans wouldn't stop cheering until the player came out of the dugout and tipped his cap.

"The 1977 season was a fantastic season," Lemon said. "We hit a lot of home runs. They wouldn't let us sit down until we came out. We did set off that exploding scoreboard a lot. It was a lot of fun. We put a good show on. I was just a young kid [22]."

The team had a lot of seasoning, from Ralph Garr, Zisk, Gamble, and Clay Carroll to Wilbur Wood.

"I was, like, in awe of those guys," Lemon said. "It was a learning experience playing with guys who had a lot of experience. I was like a baby watching them play."

Lemon was not the least bit surprised how wild Sox fans were for victory. The team had not won a World Series since 1917 and had not won a pennant since 1959, and the players sensed the North Side Cubs were really kings in the city.

By the NUMBERS .302—The highest batting average compiled by a regular for the South Side Hit Men, achieved by Lamar Johnson, who split time between designated hitter and first baseman.

"We felt like we were the stepchild of the Chicago Cubs," said Lemon, whose son Marcus, a shortstop from the University of Texas, was drafted in 2006 by the Texas Rangers. "You always kind of sensed it was a Cubs town. The people [Sox fans] were just hungry for a winner."

Animal House. That's what Comiskey Park felt like to visiting players in 1977. The fans were nonstop raucous, the cheers for home players so relentless that they were forever taking curtain calls. Opposing players grew annoyed and even suggested that their hurlers hit Sox batters with pitches to teach them a lesson in humility.

"It's like the Christians and the lions all over again," Zisk said. "I don't know whether the crowd comes here to watch us or we come here to watch them. Whatever it is, it's beautiful!"

The magic ran out in 1978. Players like Zisk and Gamble, who enjoyed themselves in '77, accepted offers of richer, multi-year contracts from other teams. Veeck had bigger aspirations, but the Sox were on their way to a 71–90 finish when he fired manager Bob Lemon.

In his place, Veeck hired Larry Doby, the former All-Star outfielder, as the second black manager in baseball history. Veeck and Doby went way back. In 1947, when Jackie Robinson broke the color barrier with the Brooklyn Dodgers, Veeck was operating the Cleveland Indians. Only months after Robinson's debut, Veeck brought Doby to the majors as the first African-American player in the American League. The two men maintained a friendship. Doby was a coach with the Indians when the team chose Frank Robinson as the first black manager. Robinson fired Doby.

Veeck gave Doby the shot. Doby said, "I didn't know," that Veeck had him in mind, even when he joined him in the owner's hotel suite to talk. "We were always having meetings to discuss players and things."

Doby's promotion fulfilled a lifetime ambition, but the opportunity lasted weeks, not seasons. When Doby did not turn the Sox around, Veeck fired him in the off-season. Doby said it was the only time he felt let down by Veeck, and Veeck later second-guessed himself.

Soderholm lived through the joy ride of 1977 and suffered through the collapse of 1978.

"The attitude about us in 1977 was, 'When are they going to fade?'" Soderholm said. "It wasn't so much that we faded as Kansas City was unbelievable the last month of the season. I thought we were going to continue the excitement."

They did not. Many years passed before the Sox generated South Side Hit Men–type hysteria again. Soderholm, who said he now does most of his baseball rooting in front of the television set while eating popcorn, pictured only one way the Sox could muster 1977-level thrills again.

"I said the only thing they could do was win the World Series," Soderholm said.

Even when he had a ballclub that didn't win—or maybe especially when he had a ballclub that didn't win—Veeck's mind was whirring, inventing fresh ways to entice fans to the park. On July 12, 1979, the Sox were involved in a doozy of a promotion. That was

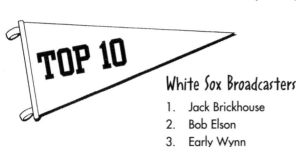

TOP 10

White Sox Broadcasters

1. Jack Brickhouse
2. Bob Elson
3. Early Wynn
4. Vince Lloyd
5. Jack Drees
6. Harry Caray
7. Jimmy Piersall
8. John Rooney
9. Ed Farmer
10. Ken Harrelson

DID YOU KNOW . . . That future Sox Cy Young Award–winner La Marr Hoyt was acquired from the New York Yankees in the 1977 trade for Bucky Dent that also brought Oscar Gamble to Chicago?

Disco Demolition Night, initiated by Mike Veeck, Bill's son, later a major and minor league baseball official.

A doubleheader was scheduled at Comiskey against the Detroit Tigers. Populist Veeck felt destroying disco records would be popular with the fans. Unfortunately, the rally became a riot. Well-known local disc jockey Steve Dahl revved up the audience of 49,000 after fans were admitted for 98 cents if they showed up with a disco record suitable for destruction.

Some records were blown up between games, as planned, but the crowd never settled down. Those in the stands still holding their records spun them onto the field. Then spectators climbed out of the seats and flooded the field. Police arrested surging fans, and the second game was forfeited to the Tigers.

"They were throwing records like Frisbees," Tigers broadcaster Ernie Harwell recalled 10 years later.

And on that musical note, the 1970s ended for the White Sox.

The Man Who Could Pitch All Night

If a pitching coach approached a young pitcher today and said, "We want you to do what Wilbur Wood did," the player would dash off into the hills and join the witness protection program. Or at least phone his agent and ask him to file a grievance.

During the 1972 season, the left-hander from Massachusetts led the team and the known world by throwing 376⅔ innings. To get Wood off the mound, you had to lasso him and drag him to the dugout. It was a throwback number, harkening back to the days of Big Ed Walsh and other pitchers from the early 1900s who, once handed the ball by a manager, approached their mound duties with the doggedness of Texas Rangers—"I'm here to do a job and I ain't quittin' till it's finished."

"I remember going back to Chicago several years ago and talking to some of the players," Wood said recently. "They were astonished. Now if someone pitches 200 innings, it's a lot. They get a $100,000 bonus for that many innings."

Wood was born in Cambridge, Massachusetts, spent his formative years in the state, and lives in a Boston suburb in retirement. When he made his major league debut in 1961 at 19 it was for the hometown Red Sox. Wood joined the White Sox in 1967 and initially was a relief pitcher. Wood's secret was the knuckleball, the floater of a pitch that befuddles batters but does not impact the shoulder or arm nearly as harshly as a curve.

"The knuckleball was the key to it for me," Wood said. "It took a lot of the stress off your arm. Sliders and curveballs put a lot of additional stress on your shoulder. The next day I was just as game as anyone else. I could recoup faster. I pitched on Sunday and I was

IF ONLY ... The line drive struck by Tiger Ron LeFlore that wrecked pitcher Wilbur Wood's left knee had missed him. Wood likely would have continued to be a 20-game winner for the Sox, put up incredible numbers for pitching stamina, and possibly would have had a career lasting eight more years.

coming back and pitching Wednesday. I was pitching with two days of rest. I stayed in a good groove."

Wood played 17 seasons in the majors and 12 were with the White Sox. He became more and more valuable, moving from a bullpen role into the starting rotation. His first big season for the Sox was 1968 when he finished 13–12 in 88 appearances. In 1969 Wood was called on 76 times and in 1970 he threw in 77 contests. He was on the TV screen more often than summer reruns.

The knuckleball makes most managers nervous. Fastballs they understand. They put a speed gun on the delivery and can clock it at Ferrari speed. Knuckleballs tend to do whatever they please, with their authors frequently admitting not even they know where they're going. White Sox manager Chuck Tanner recognized Wood as an important member of the staff, but he didn't know if his blood pressure could take Wood as his closer.

"There are several managers who don't want a knuckleballer in relief at the end of a ballgame," Wood said. "Tanner didn't want me in the bullpen. I was very happy pitching out of the bullpen."

He found true joy in the regular rotation. Wood became a full-time starter for the 1971 season and finished 22–13. He was called upon to pitch 50 percent less often, but stayed around 200 to 300 percent longer. He pitched 334 innings that year, and it turned out to be merely a warmup. In 1972 Wood's record was 24–17 with the career high 376-plus innings. In 1973 Wood's final record was an oddity, 24–20, winner and loser of 20 or more games in the same season. He threw 359⅓ innings. Wood won 20 games—20–19—for the fourth consecutive year in 1974, and his 320⅓ innings marked his fourth straight 300-inning year.

"He has three different kinds of knuckleballs," said Yankee outfielder Roy White of Wood in the 1970s. "One goes down and in to a right-handed hitter, and down and away for a lefty. Another goes up

DID YOU KNOW . . . That when Wilbur Wood (24–20) and Stan Bahnsen (18–21) each lost 20 games for the White Sox during the 1973 season, it was the first time teammates had suffered that fate in the American League since 1930?

and away to right-handed hitters and in on left-handers. And then he throws one that I don't think he knows where it's going."

For most batters, trying to hit a knuckleball was like trying to hit a butterfly.

No American Leaguer has won and lost 20 games in a season since Wood. His 376⅔ innings in a season is the most in the majors since Grover Cleveland Alexander's 388 in 1917 and his 49 starts in 1972 is second most since 1900. Jack Chesbro started 51 games for the New York Giants in 1904. Wood started his 49 despite a nine-day strike that carved games off that year's schedule. So it's no wonder Wood's numbers look cockeyed to a new generation.

To the pitcher of the 2000s, those numbers look like typographical errors. It takes only 230 innings (or less) to lead either the American League or National League these days. Pitchers are handled much more carefully and have been conditioned to feel that any time they throw many more than 100 pitches in a ballgame they are risking their future career. Once Wood won two games on the same day as a reliever. Physically, Wood did not look imposing. He more resembled David Wells, with a slight paunch. Periodically, hecklers teased Wood by calling him "pot belly," "fatty," or "beer belly." Wood joked that he needed the weight around his middle for balance. The combination of appearing comparatively doughy and employing a pitch that looked eminently hittable had to drive batters insane. They flailed at the air so often their swings tied them in knots.

"It looks like a batting practice pitch—soft, tempting," said first baseman Mike Epstein, at the time playing for the Angels.

Wood said he learned the knuckleball from his father as a junior high player, but like nearly all other pitchers tried to make the majors on the strength of his fastball.

"As fast as I could throw it," Wood said, "my fastball was a yard too short."

Knuckleballers have always been in short supply. Teams do not seek them out, but rather accept them as gifts if all else fails in the pitch repertoire.

"Most pitchers who want to come up with a knuckleball do it because they hurt their arm," Wood said. "But they started too late. I was throwing a knuckleball when I was a kid. There is no question about it, it is difficult to master."

When teams send scouts into the field, their marching orders are not to discover the next great knuckleball pitcher. They are supposed to find unhittable guys who blow smoke past the hitters.

"You take your scouts today, and all they've got is a stopwatch," Wood said. "All they want to see is 95 mph and 'we'll teach them the rest.' The secret of pitching is changing speeds and keeping the batters off-balance."

Wilbur Wood (right) poses with teammate and fellow knuckleballer Hoyt Wilhelm. Photo courtesy of the Rucker Archive.

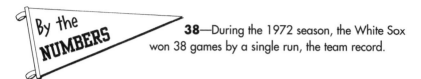

38—During the 1972 season, the White Sox won 38 games by a single run, the team record.

Wood said he had the knuckler in the mix, but still needed to fine tune it in the majors. Time spent receiving tips from Hoyt Wilhelm, the knuckleballer supreme, helped a great deal. Wilhelm told Wood he had to rely on the knuckler at least 70 percent of the time for it to become an unhittable weapon. Wood, who said maybe it was fate that he ended up on the same team as Wilhelm, said the two pitchers played catch together—throwing knuckleballs back and forth.

If a mystique surrounds knuckleball throwers—much to their advantage—they must be of rare skill, or everyone would try it. Wood became an iron man who even asked to pitch more often than on two days rest. Today pitchers start on five days rest. During the 1971 season, Tanner revealed that Wood had asked him to start against Kansas City on one day's rest.

"I said I'd see," Tanner recounted. "When the time came, I decided against it. He said, 'But you promised.' I said, 'I didn't promise. I said I'd think about it.' He was very disappointed."

Wood told Tanner that under the right circumstances, he wanted to start both games of a doubleheader. He had an easy throwing game against the New York Yankees once and the day after said, "I could have pitched the second one. I'd like to try it sometime." Tanner's response? "I'll think about it." Wood did start both games of a doubleheader at Yankee Stadium in 1973.

One of Wood's prime supporters in the hierarchy was pitching coach Johnny Sain. Sain saw no reason why Wood couldn't start with two days rest. He understood that the knuckleball's properties would not tax Wood's arm.

"He's an amazing man," Sain said. "He doesn't let anything bother him. Not everybody can do it the way Wilbur does. He has the perfect temperament. He just never gets rattled, that's all."

Except for 1972, when the White Sox finished second in the American League West Division, the team won just enough games during Wood's best years to give fans hope.

"We were winning ballgames," Wood recalled. "We were in contention. We had great fan support."

Many pitchers simply wear out with time, their bodies, their arms especially, aging to the point where they can no longer get men out. Given Wood's reliance on the knuckler and the free and easy motion he used to throw it, it often seemed he could play on well into his forties, much like his mentor Wilhelm. But bad luck did him in. During the sixth inning of a game against the Detroit Tigers on May 9, 1976, a line drive off the bat of Ron LeFlore cracked into Wood's left knee. The force of the hit knocked him down and fractured the patella.

Wood was out for the season. While he did play two more seasons for the Sox before retiring in 1978, Wood never again had a great year. He was 37.

"It tore my knee apart," Wood said of the smash.

Wood can only laugh at how pitchers are protected these days with their rare excursions into the so-called uncharted territory of 220 innings.

"Personally," Wood said when he was at his peak, "I've always thought that pitchers don't get enough work."

TRIVIA

The 1970s were not especially kind to the White Sox, with few players notching statistics that made it onto the team's top 10 lists. But one player made his mark with frequency of plate appearances. Who led the Sox in official at-bats in 1976?

Answers to the trivia questions are on page 173.

Baseball changed, however, and pitchers do less work, not more. Just because he is past his 65th birthday doesn't mean Wood's left arm couldn't handle 300 innings right now.

Winning Ugly, Hello to Fisk, Farewell to Veeck

It didn't last. The South Side Hit Men went south and so did Bill Veeck. The two developments were related. Veeck didn't have the money to hold onto his rental players, and in the end he didn't have the money to hold onto the franchise in a new era of free agency.

In early 1981 the flamboyant Veeck said good-bye to the White Sox for a second time, selling to a management group headed by Jerry Reinsdorf and Eddie Einhorn for $20 million, the same team of leaders that owns the club to this day. Always the maverick, always the outsider to the power brokers behind the scenes, Veeck signed off with good memories, a cash profit, and his feelings about the establishment unchanged.

"I didn't like the American League owners when I came into the league and I don't like them going out," Veeck said. "Of course, I'm sure the feelings of the league owners is mutual. Or reciprocal."

Veeck never bought back into baseball again. He became estranged from the new White Sox owners and during the latter days of his life was a regular sitting with fans in the bleachers at old Wrigley Field, where it had all begun for him. Veeck died from complications of his numerous ailments at age 71 in 1986.

As it so happened, baseball did not dislike Veeck as much as he thought it did. In the summer of 1991 Veeck was inducted into the Baseball Hall of Fame in Cooperstown. Although it was just another ceremony he never would have worn a tie for, his widow Mary Frances aptly summed up the likely Veeck reaction. "I know Bill is very, very pleased," she said. "Not to mention astounded."

Veeck departed with the White Sox on the verge of rebuilding into one of the franchise's best clubs since 1959. Future Hall of Fame

TOP 10

White Sox Players Born in the Chicago Area

1. Phil Cavarretta
2. Ed Farmer
3. Bob Kennedy
4. Milt May
5. Ray Schalk
6. Tim Stoddard
7. Bill Skowron
8. Sammy Esposito
9. Ron Kittle
10. Ted Kluszewski

catcher Carlton Fisk signed as a free agent after leaving the Boston Red Sox, and he embarked on an equally memorable second chapter of his career. Tony LaRussa began his managing career. Harold Baines, one of the most popular and successful Sox players, broke in.

By 1983 things were in place for a giddy run. The Sox compiled a 99–63 record and won the West Division by 20 games. Pitcher La Marr Hoyt, coming off a 19–15 campaign, turned in a career season, finishing 24–10 and winning the American League Cy Young Award.

"I remember stepping into territory I had never been before," said Hoyt recently, who lives in South Carolina. "When you're young and things are going good and start going your way, you don't analyze it much."

Hoyt, who celebrated his 51st birthday on New Year's Day 2006, said a young ballplayer develops the feeling that things will roll along forever. In his case, it was easy to see why since the bearded, 6'1", 250-pound right-hander went 15–2 after the All-Star break.

"There was great camaraderie between the players," Hoyt said. "On the field and off the field Tony [LaRussa] was a great communicator. If you've got a manager like that, you want to knock down a wall to win for [him]."

The White Sox won 87 games the year before, but few saw pennant-winning potential. The team won close games, came from

DID YOU KNOW . . . That the 25-inning game between the White Sox and Milwaukee Brewers May 8–9, 1984, was the longest game in American League history? The White Sox won 7–6 on a Harold Baines home run. Nearing the end of his Hall of Fame career, Tom Seaver claimed the win.

behind, seemed to win on days it had no chance to win. The results perplexed Texas Rangers manager Doug Rader who suggested that the good times would end for the Sox any day. "They're winning ugly," Rader noted.

At first insulted, the White Sox and their fans adopted the comment as a battle cry, as a badge of honor. As is often said in team sports, it doesn't matter if you look pretty winning, the main thing is to win. Hoyt said the Sox were a loose bunch.

"We had a fun time on and off the field," he said. "Tony had a suite and we sat around with food and beers and talked baseball. When you've got guys around who are talking baseball, good things are going to come out of it. That was probably the most fun I ever had in one year."

Hoyt spent eight years in the majors, ending in 1986, and had a lifetime record of 98–68. He became the American League's first million-dollar pitcher when he signed a six-year contract in 1984. In a controversial move (though the key man from the other side was future managerial icon Ozzie Guillen), the White Sox traded Hoyt after a 13–18 1984 season, and he injured his shoulder with the San Diego Padres. Complications from the injury and substance abuse cut short his career. Hoyt was estranged from the Sox for a period, but they reconciled and he attends SoxFest events and has helped out in spring training. The Cy Young Award was the highlight of his pitching career.

"That's what I'm most associated with," said Hoyt, who sells golf equipment at a sporting goods store and said fans remember him. "I hear them say, 'He used to play baseball. He won the Cy Young Award.'"

The White Sox did not mess around that season, maintaining a big lead in the standings. Still, the Kansas City Royals harbored hope of making hay during a late series in Chicago.

"To me," Hoyt said, "the highlight of that season was September. I said, 'When they leave, they're going to be 14 games behind. I'm going to shut them out, and if they score during the weekend here, they'll be lucky.' I shut them out."

When he was a kid, Hoyt said he imagined being on the mound and pitching so well in front of friendly fans that they called his name. During the Kansas City game, lost in his own zone of excellence, Hoyt kept firing strike after strike until a sound penetrated his thoughts.

"I heard this roar from the crowd," Hoyt said. "I'm standing out there and just paying attention to what I'm supposed to do. I have a one-hitter going, a shutout. I remember toeing the rubber and I heard this sound. The whole stadium was going, 'La Marr!' I was so into concentrating. All I was watching was Carlton Fisk's knees [for the sign to be put down]. But the whole stadium was calling my name. Boom! Boom! It was so loud they were actually bouncing me off the mound. That is what I heard when I was eight or nine years old. I knew it was destiny that I would shut them [the Royals] out."

That season was something special, Hoyt said, for the team and for him.

"I was as hot as I've ever been in my life," he said.

The White Sox won the division, but could not advance, losing three games to one to the Baltimore Orioles. Hoyt recorded the only victory, 2–1.

The Winning Ugly Sox label endured in fan memory long after the team was broken up. T-shirts commemorating the season helped. In fact, 20 years later, LaRussa, then managing the St. Louis Cardinals, admitted that he still owned two of them. Good souvenirs for the field boss who was named Manager of the Year.

An unexpected boost was provided in 1983 by outfielder Ron Kittle, who swatted 35 home runs and drove in 100 runs to capture the Rookie of the Year award. Kittle had appeared in 20 games in 1982 and was an unknown quantity. Kittle played so well he was selected for the All-Star team, and even better, the 50th anniversary game was held at Comiskey Park. Kittle said he spent much of his time at the event collecting autographs from the bigger-name stars.

Years later he wrote a book highlighting that season called *Ron Kittle's Tales from The White Sox Dugout*. The winning ugly phrase "wasn't as catchy as 'Remember the Alamo,'" Kittle said, but it worked for the Sox.

Like Hoyt, Kittle recalled 1983 as a special time, saying he acquired "a lifetime of memories in just one season. Winning was what we needed around here [Chicago]."

Tom Seaver did not make the Hall of Fame on the strength of his 2½ seasons with the White Sox, but he did add 33 wins to his lifetime total between 1984 and 1986.

Carlton Fisk's time with the Sox did enhance his Hall credentials, however. Although he entered the Hall of Fame in a Red Sox cap after a 24-year career that kept him in the big leagues until he was 45, Fisk was probably secretly wearing one white sock and one red sock. He pretty much experienced a half-and-half career.

Fisk grew up in New England, made his Red Sox debut in 1969, and joined the White Sox in 1981, staying in uniform until 1993. He wanted to stay longer, and after the White Sox released Fisk in June, he and the team for years stayed farther apart psychologically than geographically, since the player still resided in the area.

The prototypical hard-nosed field leader set a record for home runs by a catcher and most games played by a catcher. His No. 72 uniform jersey was retired in 1997, and ultimately Fisk had a statue of him constructed at the new Comiskey Park.

TRIVIA

Who replaced Carlton Fisk as the White Sox starting catcher in 1992?

Answers to the trivia questions are on page 173.

"I can't say I've been liked by everybody, but I'm always prepared to play the game and I think I'm respected as a professional," Fisk said once while still active.

Fisk had the aura of a winner, the determination of a never-give-up guy, could carry a team on his shoulders, and could almost will teammates to play better.

One reason the player nicknamed "Pudge" sustained his longevity in the sport's most demanding position was his adherence to a rigid off-season training program, including weightlifting, particularly after an injury in 1984. Given the attention paid to players'

Carlton Fisk spent the second half of his Hall of Fame career in a White Sox uniform. Photo courtesy of Getty Images.

By the NUMBERS **1,743**—Total games one-time Sox shortstop and future manager Ozzie Guillen played for the team between 1985 and 1997.

involvement with steroids and their body-building techniques nearly 20 years later, it is ironic that during the 1986 season a Kansas City newspaper story could write of an unusual Sox practice, "hold your breath, baseball—weightlifting." Chicago was actually paying a conditioning coach who (horrors) made dietary recommendations (oh, my), too. The long-held notion that weightlifing would make baseball players' muscles lose flexibility was dying.

As a player, and even in his rare post-retirement pronouncements, Fisk came to symbolize old-fashioned baseball values. He projects the image of a highly competitive man willing to sacrifice to win and a leader who demands excellence. He feels strongly about baseball traditions and wants to see young newcomers respect the game. In some ways, Fisk resembles the Kevin Costner character Crash Davis in the movie *Bull Durham*. Only Fisk was more successful.

"You have to wonder," Fisk speculated in a 1993 interview, "if there's anybody to pass the torch to."

A New Comiskey and Some New-Looking White Sox

If you build it, they will stay.

The lobbying, the politicking, the planning, and the charges of selling out fans were intense, lengthy, and ultimately led to the construction of a new Comiskey Park. The grand palace of baseball was showing its age in the 1980s, and the Reinsdorf ownership group wanted it replaced. Or else. Reinsdorf said the team needed a new ballpark in order to compete financially.

The "or else" would be the relocation of the team, the abandoning of the South Side of Chicago for somewhere else. Would you believe, St. Petersburg? The good fathers of the Tampa Bay area did build a ballpark on faith, believing for sure that the major leagues would come.

An engineering study released in June 1986 concluded that Comiskey Park was gradually disintegrating, and it made more sense to build a new ballpark than renovate and repair. Only the season before, the team hosted 11 fans who attended the first game played at Comiskey on July 1, 1910. By February 1986, the White Sox announced they would not play at Comiskey beyond the 1988 season, and unless a new stadium was built the team would look for a new home. It took passage of a bill in the Illinois legislature on a stopped-clock vote past midnight of June 30 leading into July 1 to authorize spending for a new Comiskey Park. The action saved the White Sox for Chicago.

Comiskey was the oldest park in the majors at the time, and there had not been a new park built in some time. The last building splurge had produced a spate of circular, cookie-cutter stadiums like Atlanta–Fulton County Stadium, Three Rivers Stadium in

IF ONLY . . . The White Sox had kept Sammy Sosa. The future slugger was peddled across town in a trade to the Chicago Cubs with pitcher Ken Patterson for outfielder George Bell on March 30, 1992. Sosa became the first player in baseball history to crack more than 60 home runs in a season three times.

Pittsburgh, and Riverfront Stadium in Cincinnati, arenas where both football and baseball teams cohabited. The Sox and their architects did not know they were in the forefront of a stadium construction boom that would produce a more retro look, a series of single-use facilities that harkened back in flavor to baseball of the past while providing first-class amenities of the present.

In 1989, when the new Comiskey was only partially complete—across the street from the old one—it was hailed as an exciting project with luxury boxes, elevators, and unobstructed seating. Part owner Eddie Einhorn announced, "This will be the premier facility in baseball. None of this artificial turf and domes."

Nostalgic good-byes were paid to the original Comiskey in 1990, with ceremonies and fanfare, and heralded a new beginning in a spanking new building for the 1991 season.

"I hate to see the old park go," said Hall of Famer Luke Appling. "There's always mixed feelings when you have to tear down something. But I guess it's like me, getting old."

The new park opened April 18, 1991, and the Sox lost 16–0 to the Detroit Tigers. It had been 18 years since the completion of another baseball-only stadium in Kansas City. Sox starter Jack McDowell was shelled. In some ways, the game foreshadowed the soon rocky relationship between fans and the park. While Sox administrators had their hearts in the right place trying to build a new baseball palace, Comiskey soon became as controversial as another Chicago landmark—the Picasso sculpture adorning downtown.

Other new ballparks sprouted, and it was apparent that more care was taken in shaping their baseball atmosphere. The upper decks at Comiskey were too steep. Fans complained that the building seemed sterile, more like checking into an Embassy Suites chain hotel. The shine wore off quickly and negative reviews were splashed around the nation.

Certainly helped by the curiosity factor, the White Sox drew a record attendance of 2,934,154 fans, the mark the defending World Series champs eclipsed with 2,957,414 customers in 2006. But with sluggish performance on the field over many seasons, and growing disenchantment with the stadium—especially with revered, funky old Wrigley Field across town for comparison—crowds shrunk.

Dismayed over the disgruntlement, Sox management fine-tuned the park, seeking to find the proper ambience. Tweaking did not seem to do the trick, but each minor change represented improvement. Finally, in 2003, the White Sox signed a deal for naming rights.

Scott Fletcher, a 1980s Sox shortstop whose career extended into the early 1990s, and is a cousin of Cubs catcher Michael Barrett, said there were dramatic differences between the two Comiskey Parks.

A visitor sits in the outfield seats in the steep upper deck of the new Comiskey Park in April 1991.

141

That current White Sox manager Ozzie Guillen won a Gold Glove at shortstop for the team in 1990?

"Old Comiskey had tradition and a lot of great players played there," Fletcher said. "[The new one], it was a little bit different. It was a little bit like a new era. Gosh, the new clubhouse was about the length of the left-field line. The new Comiskey was a great ballpark. It was a great year. Every time you move into a new park, there is so much excitement."

The Comiskey name was lost in the sponsorship transaction that followed as the park became U.S. Cellular Field, but $68 million from the phone company was earmarked for alterations and upkeep. This time the improvements were dramatic. The highest rows of seats in the upper deck were removed and the top of the stadium reshaped. A grassy area in center field was added. The park was transformed from a drab facility into a fan-friendly park. The reputation of Comiskey (which many fans insisted on calling the renovated structure anyway) was greatly enhanced.

Patricia Bullock of Hinsdale, Illinois, however, made clear she was unhappy with the official name change—Bullock was Charles Comiskey's granddaughter. However, in April 2004, the White Sox dedicated a statue to the team founder that stands on the center-field concourse. At the unveiling ceremony, Jerry Reinsdorf called the statue "a fitting tribute to the old gentleman" and said, "It's an honor to be the person to temporarily carry the torch he lit in 1901."

If the building of a new park was a brick-and-mortar upgrade, the near-simultaneous arrival in the majors of a powerful first baseman named Frank Thomas engendered nearly as much happiness. Thomas was the Sox player of the decade in the 1990s, and he earned the nickname "the Big Hurt" from the thumping he put on opposing teams. He hit home runs, drove in big runs, hit for average, and had a sharp enough batting eye to accumulate 100 walks a season, too.

By the time Thomas departed for the Oakland A's for the 2006 season, he was regarded as the all-time best White Sox player.

Thomas knew his statistics, but didn't think there was anything wrong with that.

"This is an individual sport," he said. "It's played as a team, but no one can swing for you. No one can pitch for you. There's nothing wrong with talking about numbers."

When baseball people talked about numbers and Thomas's name in the same sentence, it was usually in connection with how they would carry him to the Hall of Fame.

Righty Jack McDowell pitched more effectively on other days than he did the day the new Comiskey Park opened. A player known for doing things his way and for his participation with a rock-and-roll band, McDowell was the pitching staff leader in 1993 when the White Sox won their division to advance to the playoffs. He turned in his best season, winning 22 games and capturing the Cy Young Award.

Always colorful in his dealings with reporters, unfortunately a lightning rod for such things as a nightclub fight in New Orleans while hanging with Pearl Jam's Eddie Vedder (during which McDowell was knocked unconscious), and often involved in testy front-office relations, McDowell, aka "Black Jack," was a fan favorite during his 1987–1994 stay with the White Sox. He admitted he was capable of losing his cool, talking a lot, and getting into trouble because of it. He questioned the team's commitment to winning because it did not sign him to a long-term contract.

TRIVIA

What two landmark hitting feats were accomplished by 1995 White Sox players during games in September that season?

Answers to the trivia questions are on page 173.

Several years after retirement, McDowell was asked if he would prefer owning his Cy Young Award or having a number-one hit record. "I'd rather have a Cy Young because you earn that," he said. "A number-one record doesn't mean squat. All that means is you were allowed to get in there and a bunch of dummies bought your record."

McDowell, who retired in 1999, with a 127–87 lifetime record, has played music longer than he pitched.

At various times during the 1990s, the White Sox featured players who did special things. In 1990 reliever Bobby Thigpen saved a team and major league record 57 games. Thigpen, who appeared in a career high 77 games that season, grew up in Aucilla, in North Florida, watermelon country. As a 12-year-old, he thought he was rich because he made $6 a day baling hay.

Years later, Thigpen said he could have saved 60 games that memorable season, "I blew eight saves and five of them were with a three-run lead. Typical, you come in with a big cushion and just throw it down the middle."

Most of the greatest seasons third baseman Robin Ventura enjoyed during his 16-year major league career came with the White Sox. Ventura played on the 1993 division winners. He smashed nearly 300 home runs and drove in close to 1,200 runs, but Ventura is best remembered as a six-time Gold Glove winner (five with the Sox) and phenomenal clutch hitter who struck 18 grand slams (third most in major league history).

During his 2004 final season, Ventura was asked why he was so great with the bases loaded. "Mostly luck, I guess," he said, underestimating his own ability. Ventura, who overcame a horrible ankle break in spring training 1997 on a slide into home plate and left the White Sox for a four-year, $32 million, free-agent deal with the Mets, went public with his feelings for the team when he retired. "I will always feel like I'm a White Sox," he said.

Injury played a major role in the career of another potential star. Bo Jackson, a star in the National Football League and an impact player with the Kansas City Royals, never played a full season for the Sox in 1991, 1992, or 1993.

A spectacular athlete and a rare success at the pro level in two sports, Jackson had speed and panache, and he could play. Jackson, who makes his home in the Chicago area, rebounded from hip replacement surgery, to a point. He hit 16 home runs for the Sox in 1993, but never got into more than 85 games in a season.

The White Sox envisioned Jackson as a possible gate attraction and a potentially devastating designated hitter if he could not run at full speed when they signed him for the apparent bargain price of

By the NUMBERS **4-2**—The final result in games in the 1993 American League Championship Series, when the Toronto Blue Jays defeated the White Sox in their first postseason showing in a decade.

$700,000 in April 1991. Jackson was not even expected to suit up until 1992, but played in 27 games in '91.

As well-known for his Nike commercials as his on-field exploits, Jackson had a major following because of his knack for the dramatic and the division of his talents between football and baseball. Jackson's return to the diamond defied the odds and medical science, and no one really knew how long his surgically mended hip would hold up. But Bo knew baseball and Bo knew the limits of his own body.

After missing 18 months of play, on his first swing with an artificial hip, Jackson hit a home run into the right-field stands at Comiskey Park. The exploding scoreboard did its thing to commemorate the occasion, one that typically Jackson rose to. A fan exchanged the ball for other signed memorabilia so Jackson could keep it for his late mother.

Jackson understood he took a risk playing baseball again but said he did it for two reasons, "Number one is for myself, and number two is for my mother."

The little miracle didn't last long, however, and sadly Jackson was retired by his 32nd birthday.

Frank Thomas

The big man sat in the visitors' dugout with a broad smile on his face. Hugs and handshakes had followed him across the diamond at U.S. Cellular Field during warm-ups. He was a familiar face in a familiar setting, but Frank Thomas wore the uniform of the Oakland A's instead of the Chicago White Sox.

It was the third week in May of a new season, the spring of 2006, months after Thomas and the only major league team he ever knew parted ways. There are no more forevers in professional team sports, and Thomas was living proof. Despite being acknowledged as the greatest player in White Sox history, Thomas was still active, playing for a new team instead of the defending world champions. And this was his debut appearance in Chicago as a member of the opposition.

"It's a different feeling walking in today," Thomas said to a crowd of reporters. "But I feel like it's coming home. I love Chicago. Chicago is home."

Thomas spent 16 years in a Sox uniform. He batted .307. He slugged 448 home runs. He collected 1,465 RBIs. He was selected as the Most Valuable Player in the American League in 1993 and 1994 and probably should have won the award one or two more times. A big man at 6'5" and 270 pounds, Thomas acquired the nickname of "the Big Hurt." And boy, did he put the hurt on enemy pitchers.

Thomas came out of Auburn University to establish himself as one of the top players of his generation. He split time between first base and designated hitter, and if not for injuries rendering him lame for the better parts of the 2004 and 2005 seasons, would probably have spent the remainder of his career with the White Sox.

Earmarked for the heart of the Sox batting order, Thomas rushed his rise to the majors when he broke in at mid-season 1990, jumping from Double A ball directly to the majors and hitting .330 in 60 games. It was an "I'm here" declaration.

Even at the beginning of Thomas's big-league career, then–White Sox hitting coach Walt Hriniak saw the future. "He uses the whole field," Hriniak said of Thomas's hitting habits. "He can go into right and center, not only for a single and double, but he has the ability to hit the ball over the fence from one line to the next. He has the potential to hit for high average and hit a lot of home runs."

Hriniak got that right. He might have added that Thomas had the best eye for separating balls and strikes in the American League since Ted Williams, collecting 100-plus walks a year.

All of the promise residing in his massive body erupted on the playing field. Talking about the White Sox of the 1990s meant talking about the Thomas decade. "It was a great 10-year run for me in the '90s," he said. "I'm proud of it." And the years of productivity spilled over into the new century, too.

In 1993, when the Sox won the West Division, Thomas hit 41 home runs, drove in 128 runs, and batted .317. The next year he stroked 38 home runs, drove in 101, and batted .353 in just 111 games in a strike-shortened season. In 1997 Thomas cracked 35 homers, drove in 125, and his .347 average led the league. During the 2000 season, when the Sox again advanced to the playoffs, Thomas hit 43 home runs, drove in 143 runs and batted .328. Thomas hit 40 home runs in a season for the Sox five times.

Thomas was blessed with the powerful build that many other baseball players sought to engineer through steroids during the 1990s and into the 2000s. Thomas spoke out loudly against drug use long before the issue truly exploded in the public eye. There was never a hint of suspicion about his physique, and that makes his career numbers stand out in bolder relief.

The Big Hurt follows through on a home run against the Seattle Mariners on July 30, 1994.

Those closest to Thomas always considered him a wonderful guy, but he had several disagreements with the White Sox front office, being outspoken when he probably should not have been, making comments about the organization, about being underpaid and underappreciated when they were more distraction than constructive. It did not help that Thomas endured a testy divorce and that family members faced difficult illnesses. If Thomas seemed superhuman at the plate, those incidents made him seem like a more fragile human being. Never, however, was there any dispute about Thomas's ability to hit the ball. Esteemed baseball writer Jerome Holtzman said, "He is among the very best hitters in baseball history." In a 1994 story, *Sports Illustrated* said Thomas had Ted Williams's eyes, Frank Howard's arms, Willie McCovey's legs, Rod Carew's hands, and Ernie Banks's smile. That pretty much retired the compliment machine.

TRIVIA

Of 20 categories listed in the Chicago White Sox media guide for career batting leaders, in how many was Frank Thomas ranked number one as of the start of the 2006 season?

Answers to the trivia questions are on page 173.

Yet in his last days in Chicago, Thomas was booed. His final two seasons were ruined by a broken foot, surgery, and reinjury, although he did contribute to the 2005 World Series run with 12 home runs in 34 games at a time when they were sorely needed.

But Thomas, who celebrated the championship with a cast on his foot, saw the Sox exercise a $3.5 million buyout clause instead of keeping him. General manager Kenny Williams said the White Sox couldn't wait to determine if Thomas would be healthy. Instead, Williams made a deal to acquire a new DH, Jim Thome. Thomas was a free agent. Thomas ripped Williams. Williams ripped Thomas. The men left off on sour terms.

"He is the greatest hitter in White Sox history," Williams said. "At the same time, it is my responsibility to make the best decisions I can on behalf of the organization."

As pledged, Thomas returned in 2006 in shape, showing his old form in workouts. The A's signed him to a one-year, $500,000

DID YOU KNOW . . . That Frank Thomas never scored enough runs in a single season to break into the White Sox top 10 best years of production in that statistic? Johnny Mostil was number one with 135 runs in 1925.

contract that, with incentives, was valued at $2.6 million. When Thomas showed up at U.S. Cellular in May he was struggling with a .178 average, still trying to find his comfort zone. But he was gracious discussing his relationship with the White Sox.

"There's really no hard feelings," Thomas said. "What's gone is gone. This [Chicago] is a special place in my heart. My biggest moment was leaving here as a world champion. Everyone thought I was done after last year. It's a medical miracle. I worked my butt off to come back. I always felt I would have been fine here. I wanted to retire here with the White Sox. It didn't work out. I spent 16 years here. It's a long, long time. There's no bitterness in my heart."

Thomas was relaxed and smiling, resplendent in his strange green-and-yellow A's hat.

"I really wanted to come back and prove I was healthy again and help them win a second one," Thomas said of defending the 2005 title. "Old players move on."

At that point in the season, Thomas still wasn't sure what his comeback would be like. He hoped for big things and expected to play long enough to swat his 500th homer.

"I'm not looking for a .330 average," he said. "But in the .270 range and to be a legitimate threat. I hope I can come back and do something."

Before the game, someone in the crowd held up a sign reading "We Miss Big Frank." The White Sox delivered a tribute to his Chicago career on the center-field video board between the first and second innings.

The video showed Thomas highlight plays, flashed old newspaper headlines and magazine covers, and the message, "Thanks Frank." The tribute was classy and the applause hearty. When Thomas was introduced as the next batter, he received a standing ovation, and he raised his green batting helmet in thanks.

Then, on a 3–1 count, Thomas swung and smashed the ball deep to left field. It cleared the fence and landed 402 feet away. Home run. And for the only time all season, U.S. Cellular fans offered a standing ovation to an opposing player scoring on their team.

With a dramatic sense of showmanship, clutch hitting, and appreciation of the occasion, Thomas added another home run and a single that day. The performance kick-started a terrific season, where just as in old times Thomas put up homers in the 40 range and RBIs in excess of 100. By the end of the year Thomas was being talked about not only as the American League's Comeback Player of the Year, but perhaps the Most Valuable Player.

The Big Hurt left Chicago with hurt feelings, but when he left the city in May he left behind a trail of bruised baseballs. Thomas showed he was still very much a legitimate threat.

Fans and Suffering

Bob Vanderberg was 58 years old when he was asked how long he had been a White Sox fan.

"Since before I was born," he said. "I think it's in the male line in my family. It's like the sons of Russian princes have hemophilia."

Somehow it is appropriate that Vanderberg couched his family allegiance in terms of disease. For to be a White Sox fan from the Black Sox Scandal of 1919 until 2005 was in some ways consistent with long-standing illness. After all, the Sox played every season in the American League between 1917 and 2005 without winning a World Series. Eighty-eight years' worth of near-misses, close calls, embarrassing back-of-the-pack finishes, and generations of fans going from cradle to grave without seeing the title trophy hoisted.

Vanderberg, who grew up in Oak Park, Illinois, works as an editor in the sports department of the *Chicago Tribune*, and has written books about the Sox. He knows the history inside-out, and he knows the frustration from the standpoint of personal commitment. He was 11 years old in 1959 when the Sox won their first American League pennant in 40 years and advanced to the World Series.

"I watched the World Series on TV," he said. "It was a concept so foreign to us. It was like the World Series was the Yankees' birthright. Oh, I was convinced they [the Sox] would win the next year, too."

He was also convinced the White Sox would win the pennant in 1964, 1967, and 1972.

"A lot of fans point to championships that are would-have-beens," Vanderberg said.

TOP 10

White Sox Number One Draft Picks (Since Draft Began in 1965)

1. Frank Thomas, 1989
2. Carlos May, 1966
3. Harold Baines, 1977
4. Jack McDowell, 1987
5. Robin Ventura, 1988
6. Joe Borchard, 2000
7. Brian Anderson, 2003
8. Josh Fields, 2004
9. Lance Broadway, 2005
10. Ken Piesha, 1965

Chicago is a city with two major league baseball teams: the American League South Side White Sox and the National League North Side Cubs. Few fans acknowledge the teams equally. The division is more pronounced than geographic location. Sox fans have long hated Cubs fans and Cubs fans hate Sox fans and never the twain will meet for millions of them.

Tom Bolbot of Libertyville, Illinois, who turned 50 in 2006, said he grew up on the South Side and rode the bus past Comiskey Park during his high school years. His brothers and in-laws wooed him into their fan group and they became season ticket holders for a while a decade ago.

"We went through the rough times and the good times and the almost-playoff times," Bolbot said. "Carlton Fisk was always one of my favorites. And Bill Melton. And Dick Allen. I really became a Sox fan when I was about 10 years old and in the Cub Scouts. I won an autographed White Sox baseball in a drawing. I think it's from the 1959 World Series team. I can make out about three-quarters of the signatures.

"It was just amazing when they won the World Series. It's been a long time since we had a champion in the city. It was a lot of fun. It

IF ONLY . . .
The White Sox played up to their capabilities in the 2000 American League Division Series against the Seattle Mariners. The White Sox were swept, three games to none, and in the third game lost 2–1 on a throwing error in the ninth inning.

really got the whole city excited. Those opportunities don't come along that often."

Hal Vickery, a member of the board of directors of the 232-member Windy City Sox Fans White Sox fan club, said he became a Sox supporter in 1955 at the age of five while playing outside in the backyard in Bradley, Illinois. His grandparents lived two doors down, and his grandfather was following a broadcast when shortstop Chico Carrasquel hit a home run.

"I could hear Jack Brickhouse going berserk," Vickery said. "And I ran home yelling, 'Carousel hit a home run!'"

Close, but no difference. Vickery, now a teacher who lives in Joliet, evolved into a serious Sox fan, and lived with the close calls and the occasional damnation of the team because of the Black Sox.

"I don't believe in curses," Vickery said. "But if ever a team was cursed, this one was. My grandpa was a lifelong White Sox fan, and he told me all the stories."

The Sox fan club raises thousands of dollars annually for charity through luncheons, raffles, a patio party at the park, and the like. Vickery is an "Ozzie Plan" 13-game season ticket holder and said the team's 2005 playoff run to the World Series title was the most fun he's had in his life.

"All I remember is letting out a big whoop," Vickery said of the moment-of-truth triumph over the Houston Astros. "I just couldn't believe it. My eyes watered during the trophy presentation. It was, 'After 50 years, finally.'"

The despised Cubs gained the upper hand in attendance over the last 25 years despite only rarely fielding contending teams. White Sox fans have complained of being slighted on media attention, but they have not been as loyal as Cubs fans in times of despair. It has been more of a struggle for the White Sox to fill Comiskey Park and U.S. Cellular Field to the rafters.

The first million-plus attendance figure in team history was in 1951 when 1.3 million spectators turned out. That record was topped by the pennant-winning 1959 team that attracted 1.4 million, and then the 1960 bunch brought in 1.6 million fans. The Winning Ugly Sox of 1983 was the first team to entice more than 2 million fans to Comiskey. The 2005 Series champs sold 2.3 million tickets.

A consistent source of joy for White Sox fans is the organ music played by Nancy Faust. Seated in a glass booth above the 100 level behind the plate, Faust plays the tunes the whole world loves. Since 1969, she has serenaded players with tiny pieces of songs that apply

Empty seats are plentiful at Comiskey Park during a game against the Toronto Blue Jays on May 29, 2001. The White Sox ownership group, headed by Jerry Reinsdorf, evoked the disappointment of fans in 1991 when it built the unpopular stadium with the help of public funding.

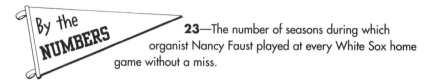

By the **NUMBERS**

23—The number of seasons during which organist Nancy Faust played at every White Sox home game without a miss.

to their names, prompted the crowd with "Charge!" music, and entertained fans with a vast repertoire of songs. Slender and blonde, Faust barely seems to have aged since she began banging out the tunes at 22. Although the White Sox have limited her music more frequently for other louder fan amusements, Faust is an institution for Sox fans.

"My whole life is identified by this place and the friendships I've made here," Faust said in a newspaper interview in 2004. "And what a great life it has been."

And that was before the White Sox won the World Series.

One thing the World Series victory did was engender fresh debate over whether Chicago would become a White Sox town, eclipsing the Cubs' apparent rule. Bruce Levine, the quarter-century Chicago baseball radio reporter affiliated with ESPN, said age groups as well as geography play a part in White Sox or Cubs allegiances.

"It's an inexact science," Levine said, giving credit to the Cubs' connection to WGN's superstation for a boost in the team following. "Cable TV came to be important to young people. It was no longer running home from school to watch the last three innings. The lifestyle changed.

"If you're 45 or older, you're either one or the other [Sox or Cubs fan]. Now that they play each other [six times in the regular season], I don't know if anyone can be passionate about both teams. Most of my friends raise their kids by the team they have a passion for. The general sports fan is interested in the team that's doing well."

Vanderberg said one often-overlooked aspect of Cubs ascension was the mistake the White Sox made permitting the late Harry Caray to transport his broadcast persona across town.

"I think there was an inferiority complex on the South Side [from not winning]," Vanderberg said. "But I could never figure that out. It seems the Sox front office had an inferiority complex, too. The Sox fans will lose interest in a losing club and just not go out. The Cubs fall out of contention right away like they usually do, but the fans still come out to the park."

After a World Series championship in 2005, after an 88-year wait, White Sox fans definitely feel superior to Cubs fans who haven't enjoyed a Series title since 1908.

"[The inferiority complex is] probably not there anymore since the Sox are world champions," Vanderberg said. "The world champion Sox," he repeated. And he smiled.

World Champs

The White Sox started fast, fooled all of the people all of the time, and finished fast, trashing the Boston Red Sox, the Los Angeles Angels, and Houston Astros in the postseason, culminating a six-month run of excellence in 2005 that left Chicago delirious with its grandest baseball celebration in decades.

The team nobody expected to win erupted out of the gate in April, led the American League Central Division all summer long, then after briefly faltering near the end of the regular season, pounded one opponent after another to walk away with the World Series trophy. They called it Ozzie Ball, after Venezuelan manager Ozzie Guillen, the one-time star shortstop who returned to lead the struggling team out of the wilderness and into paradise.

Guillen said what he thought, meant what he said, kept a loose clubhouse, played his hunches more than the percentages, and rode a starting pitching staff that brought back memories of the 1954 Indians and a starting lineup that brought back memories of the 1961 Yankees all the way to glory as the nation marveled.

"World Series Champion Chicago White Sox." It was a phrase that had not been uttered in 88 years. It was a statement that could not be exclaimed since before the end of World War I. It was a sentence that dazzled in its simplicity, but could never be overvalued in meaning.

First the White Sox swept the 2004 defending champion Red Sox in the American League Division Series by scores of 14–2, 5–4, and 5–3. Catcher A. J. Pierzynski, a new face who made an impact at bat, in the field, and with spirited play that frequently annoyed the opposition, crushed two homers in the opener. Next, Japanese import,

TOP 10

Great Things About the Sox 2005
Championship Season

1. Paul Konerko hit 40 home runs and accumulated 100 RBIs.
2. Pablo Ozuna stole home plate in a September game against Kansas City.
3. Left-handed batters hit just .105 against reliever Bobby Jenks.
4. Reliever Dustin Hermanson converted 87.2 percent of his save attempts before being injured.
5. Third baseman Joe Crede's .971 fielding percentage was only .002 off the league lead.
6. Relief pitcher Neal Cotts surrendered just one home run in 69 appearances.
7. Outfielder Scott Podsednik's 59 stolen bases were the second most in White Sox history.
8. Manager Ozzie Guillen was elected American League Manager of the Year.
9. Pitcher Mark Buehrle's 236⅔ innings was the most in the American League.
10. Freddy Garcia won all three of his playoff and World Series starts on the road, the first time that had occurred in nine years.

second baseman Tadahito Iguchi, another of general manager Kenny Williams's astute gambles, banged a three-run homer for the key blow. In the finale, first baseman Paul Konerko, the old reliable of the lineup, cracked a tie-breaking two-run homer. White Sox fans chanted "Paulie!"

Guillen had been hailed as a genius during the summer-long domination. Once the Sox began making noise in the playoffs, Guillen was no longer considered a run-of-the-mill genius. He graduated to Einstein territory.

"You can't be a manager and be afraid to make mistakes or worry about what people are going to say," Guillen explained. "A lot of managers are scared of losing their jobs. They want to please the fans. They want to please the owners. They want to please the media. All of a sudden they're not pleasing the one group they should be pleasing—the players. You have to go by your guts and believe in your players."

Known for his passion and desire to win as a player, Guillen reinforced his image by admitting he sometimes vomited in his office when the Sox lost. He spoke only of larger goals, of winning all the time. By going against the grain, by making jokes, by winging it with his feelings instead of a by-the-book, straight-laced approach, somewhere along the way over the summer of 2005, Guillen morphed into a cult figure. He was the subject of a *Playboy* interview. He made magazine covers galore, even of non-sports publications. His grinning mug was all over television sets in Chicago. Guillen's occasional spats with a former player or a journalist left some shaking their heads, but people said that was just "Ozzie being Ozzie." Guillen abruptly became more popular than Mayor Richard M. Daley, more popular than The Second City comedy club, maybe even more popular than ex-Bears coach Mike Ditka.

"I made the games fun," Guillen told *Playboy*. "People take this game so seriously now. It's not fun for them, it's work. I look at these kids now and think, 'Wow, these people don't have fun playing this game.' And you don't even know how long you'll be playing. They're going to regret it when they're done."

Guillen made things fun for the White Sox family and the whole city. The Sox finished 99–63. They regularly made comebacks. They won one-run games. They embraced the tune "Don't Stop Believin'" by the rock band Journey and made it their theme song.

Former White Sox watched intently as the organization they once represented moved toward its first World Series appearance since 1959.

"It was fantastic," said retired pitcher Billy Pierce. "It's great to see."

After disposing of the Red Sox, the White Sox opened the seven-game American League Championship Series versus the Angels with a 3–2 loss. Pierce threw out the ceremonial first pitch in that game. Then the White Sox swept the Angels four straight.

There was a different hero every night. Southpaw Mark Buehrle polished off L.A. 2–1 on a five-hit, 99-pitch complete game, and third

By the NUMBERS 52-22—The 2005 White Sox regular-season record versus the Central Division. The Sox owned the Kansas City Royals, Minnesota Twins, Cleveland Indians, and Detroit Tigers.

baseman Joe Crede knocked in the winning run with a double in the ninth inning in Game 2. In the 5–2 victory in Game 3, Jon Garland pitched another complete game and first baseman Paul Konerko went 3-for-4 with three RBIs. Freddy Garcia dominated on the mound in Game 4's 8–2 triumph, and both Pierzynski and Konerko homered.

Then it was Jose Contreras's turn to pitch a complete game in the 6–3 series clincher. Konerko, the MVP of the championships, swatted an RBI double in the ninth, and Crede's slow single up the middle pushed across the winning run an inning earlier. After a slow start, Contreras blitzed through September with a 6–0 mark and a 1.99 earned-run average. Four straight complete games by the starters.

"That's something you're never going to see again," Pierzynski said.

Of course, the most riveting play of the five-game series was not a home run, a lead change, or marvelous pitching, but an accidentally-on-purpose play that you might not ever see again either, at least in such an important setting. Pierzynski was the key protagonist.

The lefty-swinging Pierzynski was at the plate in the ninth inning of the second game with Kelvim Escobar on the mound. Angels catcher Josh Paul appeared to catch what he thought was a Pierzynski swing and a miss for strike three. As Angels players began to vacate the field, Paul rolled the ball back to the mound. Only Pierzynski realized he hadn't been called out. He ran to first base and was ruled safe. The inning continued with Pablo Ozuna pinch running for Pierzynski and Joe Crede doubling him home with the winning run.

The Angels howled, but the Pierzynski dash to first stood. The play was shown over and over again, and it was never 100 percent clear if Paul trapped the ball or caught it. Pierzynski, described by many sportswriters as the mischievous class troublemaker who

DID YOU KNOW . . . That late-season closer Bobby Jenks and his
100-mph fastball spent most of the 2005 campaign at
Double A Birmingham and the Sox had no intention of
bringing him to the majors until reliever Dustin Hermanson (34 saves)
got injured?

would get on a teacher's nerves, later said philosophically, "Even when I don't do anything, I do something."

White Sox Nation was energized from coast to coast. Someone checked in with Al Lopez, manager of the 1959 squad, on the eve of the 2005 World Series. At 97, Lopez had watched the team clinch the pennant on television. "Good for the Sox," Lopez said in Tampa. "Good for Chicago." Before the end of October, the Hall of Fame catcher and long-time manager died from a heart attack. But he lived to see the Sox take home the big prize.

White Sox fans, civic fans, and general baseball fans were gleeful when the World Series returned to Chicago. Only Cubs fans kept a low profile. And the Sox delivered victories with excitement and drama.

The White Sox scored early in their 5–3 opener win that saw Houston Astros' future Hall of Famer Roger Clemens driven from the mound by an injured hamstring. Right fielder Jermaine Dye, another off-season acquisition, took his turn delivering the big hit with a first-inning home run.

The big blow in the second game, a 7–6 Sox win, was a grand slam by Konerko, but the winning blow came off the bat of leadoff hitter Scott Podsednik, who crashed a solo homer for the decisive run after not hitting a single homer during the regular season. The third game ruined Houston's morale. Lasting 14 innings and five hours and 41 minutes, with a Series record 43 players playing, the Sox triumphed 7–5 on a home run by journeyman Geoff Blum. It was by far the biggest hit of Blum's career.

Snapshots from the deciding fourth game will stay in White Sox fans' minds for a long time. Dye, who was voted the Series MVP, knocked in Willie Harris with a single in the eighth inning for the game's only run. The suspenseful 1–0 victory was punctuated with several memorable plays. Shortstop Juan Uribe dove into the left-field

Bobby Jenks and Paul Konerko start the celebration as Chicago beat the Houston Astros 1–0 to win the World Series on October 26, 2005. The White Sox won their first World Series since 1917 by sweeping the Astros.

stands to catch a pop-up in the ninth inning and then ended the game by firing a throw to first on a grounder.

As the ball plunked into Konerko's glove, reliever Bobby Jenks, the young closer brought up from the minors in the middle of the summer, leaped in the air and thrust his arms skyward. The picture was captured by a hundred photographers and became one of the symbols of the White Sox championship.

In the locker room, the Sox spilled champagne as much as drank it, lit cigars, and whooped long and loud. Owner Jerry Reinsdorf accepted the championship trophy from Commissioner Bud Selig and celebrated the fulfillment of a quarter-century-old dream. If ever there was a team championship, this one was it. Only once before had a club won the World Series without either a .300 hitter or a 20-game winner.

TRIVIA

Who was the winningest White Sox pitcher in 2005, and how many games did he win?

Answers to the trivia questions are on page 173.

"We're the perfect example of why you don't need to put together an All-Star team to win a championship," Konerko said. "You just have to peak at the right time."

A life-sized picture of Dye was installed in the Baseball Hall of Fame in Cooperstown, New York, next to a 2005 Series exhibit for the length of the 2006 season. Normally soft-spoken, Dye did not undergo a personality transplant to brag.

"It's just special for me to be thought of as MVP and become an MVP in that group," he said of his teammates.

A few days after the Sox put their stamp on the World Series for the first time in nine decades, Chicago threw a parade. It was a school day, but neither parents nor children cared. "Attending White Sox victory parade" was a better excuse than "the dog ate my homework." Up until then, it would have been equally as unbelievable.

The parade streamed through the South Side and stopped in downtown for a lovefest between team and fans. At one juncture, Konerko, who caught the ball for the final out, stepped to the microphone. Konerko pulled the game ball out of his coat pocket and said, "It's going to this man right here because he earned it."

Konerko presented the ball to a choking up Reinsdorf and gave the boss a hug. Reinsdorf, also the owner of the six-time world champion Chicago Bulls NBA franchise, said, "This is absolutely the most fantastic day in my entire life."

Jim Landis, an outfielder on the 1959 team, who attended some of the Sox postseason games, said the organization has been good to the players from that time period. But after the 2005 Series, Landis said his wife said, "Geez, Jim, they won't have us back anymore." Landis joked, "We milked it for 46 years, what do you want?"

Teams in the 2000s do not stay together long. Among those absent would be traded center fielder Aaron Rowand, long-time franchise star Frank Thomas, and Harris, whose brief moment in the Series sun was as a pinch-hitter. Harris moved on to the Red Sox organization in 2006, but collected a World Series ring for 2005.

"I was happy just to be able to contribute," Harris said of the special run-scoring memory he retains as a Series champ. "To go out and do what I did meant a lot to me."

Harris said he spent off-season time in Cairo, Georgia, where he grew up, and visited every place from the elementary school to the middle school to the high school.

"It was just fun," Harris said. "I couldn't go anywhere for a good few weeks without people asking how it was. That ring is mine. I'm proud. No one can take it away from me."

There was a lesson in Harris's World Series cameo that he said is a good one for everyone.

"Always be ready just in case you're called upon," Harris said. "In life or baseball, whatever it is."

The Year After

Perfect time to rub it in. *Nyah, nyah, nyah, we won a World Series and you didn't.* That would be a White Sox fan talking to a Cubs fan. The White Sox went without a World Series title from 1917 to 2005. The Cubs have gone without a World Series title since 1908 and are still waiting.

Shortly after the White Sox coronation, an item appeared on the Internet aimed at Cubs fans. It was simply labeled, Cubs to White Sox Conversion Form. The item said that only Cubs fans were being considered for membership in the Chicago White Sox Fan Club at that time.

An abridged version of the form follows:

1. Please indicate the last time you watched the Chicago Cubs win a pennant: A) 1945 (please leave this form at the front desk of your nursing home); or B) Have never witnessed this event.

2. Please indicate your favorite moments in Cubs history: [some choices included] Lou Brock traded to the Cardinals for Ernie Broglio in 1964; Cubs blow an eight-game lead and finish eight games behind the Mets in 1969; a black cat running in front of Ron Santo during a critical 1969 series in Shea Stadium; the College of Coaches of the early '60s.

3. Reasons you believe the Cubs have not won a World Series since 1908: The curse of the goat; Lack of managing; The curse of the goat; Lack of pitching; The curse of the goat.

Speaking of the Cubs, former major leaguer and long-time White Sox broadcaster Ken "Hawk" Harrelson said it is about time the Sox and Cubs meet in a World Series for the first time since 1906.

IF ONLY . . . In September 2006 the White Sox could have turned back the clock to September 2005 to duplicate their season-ending hot streak to move on to the playoffs for a second straight year.

"I'd like to see a Cubs-Sox World Series just so we could end the speculation once and for all," Harrelson said. "Get it over with for the next hundred years."

There was no speculation after 2005. Members of the victorious Sox team did not stop smiling during the off-season. They discovered what it was like to be a champion in demand. A. J. Pierzynski got to present a professional wrestling belt, but avoided being put in a headlock.

"It never really quieted down," outfielder Scott Podsednik said of the off-season. "I had a hernia operation, I got married, and I made appearances doing fun things. It went by fast. Two thousand and five is going to be the year I reflect on forever."

The White Sox embraced the persona of a team that gets its hands dirty doing the little things. They called themselves grinders and adopted a large number of phrases they felt illustrated the premise. Grinder Rule No. 31: "Never swing at foolish pitches unless they're foolishly belt high right down the middle." Grinder Rule No. 41: "You can't spell WIN without a few Ks." The phrases appeared on walls at the ballpark, in programs, on message boards inside the stadium, on the radio.

On opening day of 2006 against Cleveland, the Sox players were presented replica World Series trophies about five inches tall. Relief pitcher Cliff Politte, who finished 7–1 with a 2.00 earned-run average in 2005, said he knew where his was going.

"I'm having a new house built," he said, "and I'm going to have an office and keep it on my desk."

Politte said the explosion of fan interest was a change.

"When someone recognizes you, it's a neat thing," Politte said. "You also see a lot more White Sox hats downtown. And there are some people who were diehard Cubs fans who give us respect now."

Jim Thome watches his two-run homer leave the park during the fourth inning of the Sox's opening-day game against the Cleveland Indians on April 2, 2006.

Luis Aparicio was there for the trophy presentation ceremony. Billy Pierce participated. So did former player Harold Baines. Baines missed out on a Sox World Series as a player, but made up for it as a coach.

"You can't really compare," Baines said, "but it's a great feeling to be part of it when it happened. It's great for us, great for the White Sox, and great for the city. When you take 88 years to do it, you want to soak it in as long as you can."

On the second day of the season, the Sox presented World Series rings to the victors. The first 20,000 fans were given replicas, but before the on-field ceremony, Jeff Idleson of the Baseball Hall of Fame teased the Sox in their locker room. While wearing white gloves, he spread out a soft cloth on a table and showed the Sox examples of 10 recent championship rings awarded to other teams. The players and coaches gathered in a circle. It was like jewelry browsing at Tiffany's.

Manager Ozzie Guillen surveyed the goods and joked, "Wal-Mart." Then after closer inspection of the gold-and-stone rings, he added, "If you're broke, you can sell it and send your kid to college."

After Idleson folded up the baubles, the proceedings moved outside, with a table set up between the pitcher's mound and home plate. So many photographers lined up on the first-base side that one might think a presidential address was scheduled. Then dramatic music played, the center-field wall opened, and a parade of tuxedo-clad, White Sox–cap-wearing marchers carried in the rings on pillows and formed a circle around the mound. Fans provided a standing ovation, and then owner Jerry Reinsdorf and general manager Kenny Williams presented the rings—to the men who made it happen from the men who gave them the chance to.

And then the White Sox set out to win another one. Williams was not idle. Some players were gone, some new faces arrived. No deal was more important than trading for designated hitter Jim Thome. The veteran slugger, from nearby Peoria, Illinois, came to Chicago to replace Frank Thomas in the lineup. Soft-spoken, charming, almost a homebody, the 6'4", 245-pound Thome possessed similar dimensions as Thomas and, with 430 career home runs, almost as many long-ball swats.

"Any time you come to a new team, you want to be part of what they accomplished," Thome said, "part of the special thing they accomplished. There's a lot of electricity in this park. Electricity comes when you win.

"I'm close to family. It's been everything and more than I expected. It's been a lot of fun. They got me to replace Frank Thomas, a guy with a Hall of Fame career. Hey, you've got to be ready to go."

Thome was. He produced all summer, breaking the 40-home-run and 100-RBI barriers. If anything, the Sox looked better on paper than the 2005 bunch, but the results were different. The Detroit Tigers burst out of the starting gate faster than the Kentucky Derby winner, and while the Sox regularly provided thrills to a record 52 sellout crowds, they did not play with the same consistency.

There were many notable moments besides the big hits from the big guns. Paul Konerko hit more than 30 home runs and drove in more than 100 runs for the fourth time. Jermaine Dye cleared 40 homers and 120 RBIs. With newfound slugging prowess, Joe Crede gave the Sox four hittters with 30 or more homers for the first time. Crede blossomed even more at third base, bringing back memories of Brooks Robinson and Hoover vacuum cleaners. While Cubs catcher Michael Barrett was punching Sox catcher A. J. Pierzynski in the jaw because A.J. ran him over at home plate, the Sox were beating their crosstown rivals 7–0. A.J. was the innocent party. The Sox spent the better part of a Sunday besting the Red Sox 6–5 in 19 innings in July. Freddy Garcia threatened to complete a perfect game in September, but finished with a one-hitter.

The White Sox were a hot ticket. But they had their hands full after the Minnesota Twins came to life after the All-Star break. The White Sox remained in contention for a wild-card playoff spot into the last week of the season, but could not advance.

By the
NUMBERS
Millions—The number of people White Sox owner Jerry Reinsdorf believes the team made happy by winning the 2005 World Series, many of whom wrote letters or stopped him in the street merely to say, "Thank you."

DID YOU KNOW . . . When rookie Josh Fields made his debut during September of 2006, he became only the third White Sox player to hit a home run in his first at-bat?

Nobody seemed more perplexed about the difficulties Sox pitchers had and the lack of timely hitting than Guillen.

"Win or lose, it's always the manager's responsibility," Guillen said late in the season. "Last year we were winning with Ozzie Ball. This year we are losing with Ozzie Ball. I'm the face of the ballclub, and I will take the heat."

There was disappointment, but not much heat. After a Sox loss to the Cubs in 2006, a North Side fan was bragging in a men's room. "World champs, buddy!" one Sox fan retorted. "World champs!" Another Sox fan looked at the friendly stranger and shouted, "It never gets old!" And the two young men high-fived. The 2005 season will be forever prized in Sox lore.

Even at the end of the 2006 season, the rings from 2005 still glowed in the sunshine. The sweet taste of success from the first world title in 88 years lingered on fans' tongues. Yes, they all wanted more, another title—the fans, the players, the manager, all of them—but in the back of their minds the magic words "World Champion Chicago White Sox" were still fresh.

ANSWERS TO
TRIVIA QUESTIONS

Page 3: Nixey Callahan 1902; Frank Smith 1905; Frank Smith 1908.

Page 9: Big Ed Walsh led the White Sox in earned-run average six times, the best being 1.27 in 1910.

Page 18: The White Sox's longest winning streak was 19 games in 1906.

Page 25: Shoeless Joe Jackson led the 1919 White Sox with a .351 batting average.

Page 31: Jack Harshman struck out 16 batters in a 1954 game.

Page 37: Carl Reynolds hit three home runs in a 1930 game.

Page 45: The most .300 hitters the White Sox ever had in a season is five, which happened four times, in 1920, 1924, 1936, and 1937.

Page 51: The American League had 26 All-Stars in 1983. Only one of them, Ron Kittle, was a member of the White Sox.

Page 65: The highest the White Sox ever finished in the 1940s was third, in 1941.

Page 70: Counting one tie, Nellie Fox led the Sox in batting average four times during the 1950s.

Page 78: Groundskeeper Roger Bossard.

Page 83: The White Sox recorded 17 straight winning seasons between 1951 and 1967.

Page 90: Three. Nellie Fox, Sherm Lollar, and Early Wynn.

Page 102: Cy Young Award–winner Early Wynn said of the 1959 season, "The best thing of all is a winner for Chicago."

Page 106: The American League pennant-winning White Sox hit only .250 as a team in 1959.

Page 115: Gary Peters led the American League in ERA in 1963 at 2.33 and in 1966 at 1.98.

Page 119: The popular banner at Comiskey Park in 1977 read: Pitch at Risk to Rich Zisk.

Page 131: Jorge Orta led the White Sox in at-bats in 1976 with 636.

Page 136: Ron Karkovice replaced Carlton Fisk as the White Sox starting catcher in 1992.

Page 143: In a 14–3 win over Texas, Robin Ventura hit grand slams in consecutive innings. In a 14–4 win over Minnesota, Lance Johnson got a team record–tying six hits in a game, including a team record three triples.

Page 149: Frank Thomas was listed number one in 12 of 20 team batting categories as of the start of the 2006 season.

Page 164: Jon Garland was the winningest White Sox pitcher in 2005, with 18 wins.

Chicago White Sox All-Time Roster (through 2006 season)

Players who have appeared in at least one game with the Chicago White Sox.

A

Jeff Abbott (OF)	1997–2000
Jim Abbott (P)	1995, 1998
Shawn Abner (OF)	1992
Cal Abrams (OF)	1956
Fritz Ackley (P)	1963–64
Cy Acosta (P)	1972–74
Jose Acosta (P)	1922
Jerry Adair (2B)	1966–67
Bobby Adams (3B)	1955
Doug Adams (C)	1969
Herb Adams (OF)	1948–50
Grady Adkins (P)	1928–29
Jon Adkins (P)	2003–05
Tommie Agee (OF)	1965–67
Juan Agosto (P)	1981–86
Scotty Alcock (3B)	1914
Dick Allen (1B)	1972–74
Hank Allen (3B)	1972–73
Lloyd Allen (P)	1974–75
Neil Allen (P)	1986–87
Bill Almon (SS)	1981–82
Luis Aloma (P)	1950–53
Roberto Alomar (2B)	2003–04
Sandy Alomar (2B)	1967–69
Sandy Alomar Jr. (C)	2001–04, 2006
Dave Altizer (OF)	1909
Nick Altrock (P)	1903–09

Luis Alvarado (SS)	1971–74
Wilson Alvarez (P)	1991–97
Brian Anderson (OF)	2005–06
Hal Anderson (OF)	1932
John Anderson (OF)	1908
Larry Anderson (P)	1977
Mike Andrews (2B)	1971–73
Luis Andujar (P)	1995–96
Luis Aparicio (SS)	1956–62, 1968–70
Pete Appleton (P)	1940–42
Luke Appling (SS)	1930–43, 1945–50
Maurice Archdeacon (OF)	1923–25
Rudy Arias (P)	1959
Charlie Armbruster (C)	1907
Gerry Arrigo (P)	1970
Ken Ash (P)	1925
Paul Assenmacher (P)	1994
Jake Atz (2B)	1907–09
Chick Autry (C)	1929–30
Earl Averill (C)	1960

B

Stan Bahnsen (P)	1972–75
Harold Baines (OF, DH)	1980–89, 1996–97, 2000–01
Jeff Bajenaru (P)	2004–05
Floyd Baker (3B)	1945–51
Howard Baker (3B)	1914–15
Jesse Baker (P)	1911
Dave Baldwin (P)	1973
James Baldwin (P)	1995–2001

Alan Bannister (IF, OF)	1976–80	Neil Berry (2B)	1953
Floyd Bannister (P)	1983–87	Mike Bertotti (P)	1995–97
Lorenzo Barcelo (P)	2000–02	Rocky Biddle (P)	2000–02
Charlie Barnabe (P)	1927	Charlie Biggs (P)	1932
Bob Barnes (P)	1924	John Bischoff (C)	1925
Red Barnes (OF)	1930	Hi Bithorn (P)	1947
Rich Barnes (P)	1982	Jeff Bittiger (P)	1988
Salome Barojas (P)	1982–84	Bill Black (2B)	1924
Bill Barrett (OF)	1923–29	Charlie Blackburn (P)	1921
Francisco Barrios (P)	1974, 1976–81	Lena Blackburne (IF)	1910, 1912,
Cuke Barrows (OF)	1909–12		1914–15, 1927, 1929
Les Bartholomew (P)	1932	George Blackerby (OF)	1928
Earl Battey (C)	1955–59	Ossie Blanco (1B)	1970
Jim Battle (3B)	1927	Homer Blankenship (P)	1922–23
Matt Batts (C)	1954	Ted Blankenship (P)	1922–30
Frank Baumann (P)	1960–64	Bruno Block (C)	1910–12
Jim Baumer (SS)	1949	Ron Blomberg (DH)	1978
Ross Baumgarten (P)	1978–81	Lu Blue (1B)	1931–32
Johnny Beall (OF)	1913	Geoff Blum (IF)	2005
Ted Beard (OF)	1957–58	Milt Bocek (OF)	1933–34
Gene Bearden (P)	1953	Ping Bodie (OF)	1911–14
Kevin Beirne (P)	2000	Bob Boken (IF)	1934
Ollie Bejma (2B)	1939	Greg Bollo (P)	1965–66
Tim Belcher (P)	1993	Rodney Bolton (P)	1993, 1995
Gary Bell (P)	1969	Bobby Bonds (OF)	1978
George Bell (DH)	1992–93	Bobby Bonilla (OF)	1986
Kevin Bell (3B)	1976–80	Zeke Bonura (1B)	1934–37
Ralph Bell (P)	1912	Buddy Booker (C)	1968
Albert Belle (OF)	1997–98	Ike Boone (OF)	1927
Esteban Beltre (SS)	1991–92	Ray Boone (1B)	1958–59
Chief Bender (P)	1925	Joe Borchard (OF)	2002–05
Joe Benz (P)	1911–19	Frenchy Bordagaray (OF)	1934
Jason Bere (P)	1993	Pat Borders (C)	1996
Moe Berg (C)	1926–30	Glenn Borgmann (C)	1980
Boze Berger (IF)	1937–38	Babe Borton (1B)	1912–13
Joe Berger (2B)	1913–14	Thad Bosley (OF)	1978–80
Marty Berghammer (2B)	1911	Daryl Boston (OF)	1984–90
Tony Bernazard (2B)	1981–83	Billy Bowers (OF)	1949
Dennis Berran (OF)	1912	Grant Bowler (P)	1931–32
Charlie Berry (C)	1932–33	Emmett Bowles (P)	1922
Claude Berry (C)	1904	Red Bowser (OF)	1910
Ken Berry (OF)	1962–70	Bob Boyd (1B)	1951, 1953–54

Ken Boyer (3B)	1967–68	John Buzhardt (P)	1962–67
Harry Boyles (P)	1938–39	Harry Byrd (P)	1955–56
Buddy Bradford (OF)	1966–70, 1972–75, 1976	Bobby Byrne (2B)	1917
Chad Bradford (P)	1998–2000	Jerry Byrne (P)	1929
Fred Bradley (P)	1948–49	Tommy Byrne (P)	1953
Phil Bradley (OF)	1990		
Scott Bradley (C)	1986	**C**	
Tom Bradley (P)	1971–72	Leon Cadore (P)	1923
Doug Brady (2B)	1995	Bob Cain (P)	1949–51, 1954
Dave Brain (2B)	1901	Sugar Cain (P)	1936–38
Fred Bratschi (OF)	1921	George Caithamer (C)	1934
Angel Bravo (OF)	1969	Ivan Calderon (OF)	1986–90, 1993
Garland Braxton (P)	1930–31	Earl Caldwell (P)	1945–48
Jim Breazeale (1B)	1978	Nixey Callahan (OF, P)	1901–05, 1911–13
Tom Brennan (P)	1984	Johnny Callison (OF)	1958–59
Jim Breton (3B)	1913–15	Mike Cameron (OF)	1995–98
Ken Brett (P)	1976–77	Bruce Campbell (OF)	1930–32
Alan Brice (P)	1961	John Cangelosi (OF)	1985–86
Jim Brideweser (SS)	1955–56	Jose Canseco (DH)	2001
Bunny Brief (1B)	1915	Pat Caraway (P)	1930–32
Chuck Brinkman (C)	1969–74	Andy Carey (3B)	1961
Jack Brohamer (2B)	1976–77	Cisco Carlos (P)	1967–69
Jim Brosnan (P)	1963	Steve Carlton (P)	1986
Clint Brown (P)	1936–40	Eddie Carnett (P)	1944
Delos Brown (PH)	1914	Alex Carrasquel (P)	1949
Dick Brown (C)	1960	Chico Carrasquel (SS)	1950–55
Hal Brown (P)	1951–52	Cam Carreon (C)	1959–64
Joe Brown (P)	1927	Clay Carroll (P)	1976–77
George Browne (OF)	1910	Jeff Carter (P)	1991
Jack Bruner (P)	1949–50	Mike Caruso (SS)	1998–99
Warren Brusstar (P)	1982	Chuck Cary (P)	1993
Hal Bubser (PH)	1922	Raul Casanova (C)	2005
Mark Buehrle (P)	2000–06	Norm Cash (1B)	1958–59
Don Buford (3B)	1963–67	Larry Casian (P)	1998
Smoky Burgess (C)	1964–67	Carlos Castillo (P)	1997–99
Jamie Burke (C)	2003–05	Tony Castillo (P)	1996–98
Jimmy Burke (SS)	1901	Vince Castino (C)	1943–45
Ellis Burks (OF)	1993	Paul Castner (P)	1923
Bill Burns (P)	1909–10	Danny Cater (OF)	1965–66
Britt Burns (P)	1978–85	Wayne Causey (2B)	1966–68
Joe Burns (C)	1924	Phil Cavarretta (1B)	1954–55
Jim Busby (OF)	1950–52, 1955	Domingo Cedeno (IF)	1996

Jerry Dahlke (P)	1956
Bruce Dal Canton (P)	1977
Mark Dalesandro (C)	2001
Tom Daly (2B)	1902–03
Tom Daly (C)	1913–15
Pat Daneker (P)	1999
Dave Danforth (P)	1916–19
Vic Darensbourg (P)	2004
Danny Darwin (P)	1997
Jeff Darwin (P)	1996–97
Wally Dashiell (SS)	1924
Brian Daubach (1B)	2003
Joe Davenport (P)	1999
Lum Davenport (P)	1921–24
Ben Davis (C)	2004
Dixie Davis (P)	1915
George Davis (SS)	1902, 1904–09
Ike Davis (SS)	1924–25
Joel Davis (P)	1985–88
John Davis (P)	1988–89
Tommy Davis (OF)	1968
Bill Dawley (P)	1986
Dave DeBusschere (P)	1962–63
Mike DeGerick (P)	1961–62
Jose DeLeon (P)	1986–87, 1993–95
Flame Delhi (P)	1912
Jason Dellaero (SS)	1999–99
Jim Delsing (OF)	1948, 1956
Joe DeMaestri (SS)	1951
Ray Demmitt (OF)	1914–15
Drew Denson (1B)	1993
Bucky Dent (SS)	1973–76
Sam Dente (SS)	1952–53
Jim Derrington (P)	1956–57
Joe DeSa (1B)	1985
Mike Devereaux (OF)	1995
Bernie DeViveiros (SS)	1924
Al DeVormer (C)	1918
Felix Diaz (P)	2004
Mike Diaz (1B)	1988
Rob Dibble (P)	1995
George Dickey (C)	1941–42, 1946–47

Johnny Dickshot (OF)	1944–45
Bill Dietrich (P)	1936–46
Steve Dillard (2B)	1982
Bob Dillinger (3B)	1951
Miguel Dilone (OF)	1983
John Dobb (P)	1924
Jess Dobernic (P)	1939
Joe Dobson (P)	1951–53
Larry Doby (OF)	1956–57, 1959
Cozy Dolan (1B)	1903
Jiggs Donahue (1B)	1904–09
Dick Donovan (P)	1955–60
Harry Dorish (P)	1951–55
Charlie Dorman (C)	1923
Richard Dotson (P)	1979–87, 1989
Patsy Dougherty (OF)	1906–11
Tom Dougherty (P)	1904
Phil Douglas (P)	1912
Brian Downing (C)	1973–77
Doug Drabek (P)	1997
Moe Drabowsky (P)	1972
Brian Drahman (P)	1991–93
Kelly Dransfeldt (SS)	2004
Tom Drees (P)	1991
Walt Dropo (1B)	1955–58
Larry Duff (P)	1922
Dan Dugan (P)	1928–29
Gus Dundon (2B)	1904–06
Davey Dunkle (P)	1903
Mike Dunne (P)	1992
Frank Dupee (P)	1901
Ed Durham (P)	1933
Jimmy Durham (P)	1902
Ray Durham (2B)	1995–2002
Jerry Dybzinski (SS)	1983–84
Jermaine Dye (OF)	2005–06
Jimmy Dykes (3B)	1933–39

E

George Earnshaw (P)	1934–35
Ted Easterly (C)	1912–13
Vallie Eaves (P)	1939–40

Don Eddy (P)	1970–71	Dutch Fehring (C)	1934
Mike Eden (SS)	1978	Happy Felsch (OF)	1915–20
Paul Edmondson (P)	1969	Hod Fenner (P)	1921
Hank Edwards (OF)	1952	Ed Fernandes (C)	1946
Jim Joe Edwards (P)	1925–26	Alex Fernandez (P)	1990–96
Wayne Edwards (P)	1989–91	Don Ferrarese (P)	1960
Tom Egan (C)	1971–72	Clarence Fieber (P)	1932
Ike Eichrodt (OF)	1931	Josh Fields (3B)	2006
Cal Eldred (P)	2000–01	Lou Fiene (P)	1906–09
Lee Elia (SS)	1966	Pete Filson (P)	1986
Bob Elliott (3B)	1953	Steve Fireovid (P)	1985
Sammy Ellis (P)	1969	Bill Fischer (P)	1956–58
Roy Elsh (OF)	1923–25	Carl Fischer (P)	1935
Alan Embree (P)	2001	Eddie Fisher (P)	1962–66, 1972–73
Slim Embrey (P)	1923	Jack Fisher (P)	1968
Charlie English (3B)	1932–33	Carlton Fisk (C)	1981–93
Del Ennis (OF)	1959	Patsy Flaherty (P)	1903–04
George Enright (C)	1976	Tom Flanigan (P)	1954
Mutz Ens (1B)	1912	John Flannery (SS)	1977
Joe Erautt (C)	1950–51	Roy Flaskamper (SS)	1927
Chico Escarrega (P)	1982	Scott Fletcher (IF)	1983–85, 1989–91
Sammy Esposito (3B)	1952, 1955–63	Josh Fogg (P)	2001
Mark Esser (P)	1979	Marv Foley (C)	1978–80, 1982
Jim Essian (C)	1976–77, 1981	Lew Fonseca (OF)	1931–33
Art Evans (P)	1932	Chad Fonville (IF, OF)	1997
Bill Evans (P)	1949	Gene Ford (P)	1938
Red Evans (P)	1936	Tom Fordham (P)	1997–98
Carl Everett (OF)	2003–05	Brook Fordyce (C)	1999–2000
Johnny Evers (2B)	1922	Happy Foreman (P)	1924
Sam Ewing (DH)	1973, 1976	Mike Fornieles (P)	1953–56
Scott Eyre (P)	1997–2000	Terry Forster (P)	1971–76
		Tim Fortugno (P)	1995
F		George Foster (OF)	1986
Red Faber (P)	1914–33	Pop Foster (OF)	1901
Jorge Fabregas (C)	1997	Bob Fothergill (OF)	1930–32
Ferris Fain (1B)	1953–54	Keith Foulke (P)	1997–2002
Bibb Falk (OF)	1920–28	Jack Fournier (1B)	1912–17
Bob Fallon (P)	1984–85	Nellie Fox (2B)	1950–63
Bob Farley (1B)	1962	Ken Frailing (P)	1972–73
Ed Farmer (P)	1979–81	Julio Franco (DH)	1994
Kerby Farrell (1B)	1945	Tito Francona (OF)	1958
Joe Fautsch (PH)	1916	Lou Frazier (OF)	1998

Vic Frazier (P)	1931–33, 1939	Stan Goletz (PH)	1941
Marvin Freeman (P)	1996	Wilbur Good (OF)	1918
Gene Freese (3B)	1960, 1965–66	John Goodell (P)	1928
Jake Freeze (P)	1925	Billy Goodman (3B)	1958
Charlie French (2B)	1910	Jim Goodwin (P)	1948
Ray French (SS)	1924	Tom Gordon (P)	2003
Dave Frost (P)	1977	Rich Gossage (P)	1972–76
Liz Funk (OF)	1932–33	Johnny Grabowski (C)	1924–26
		Tony Graffanino (IF)	2000–03
G		Roy Graham (C)	1922–23
Frank Gabler (PH)	1938	Wayne Granger (P)	1974
Dave Gallagher (OF)	1988–90	Jimmy Grant (3B)	1942–43
Phil Gallivan (P)	1932, 1934	Lorenzo Gray (3B)	1982–83
Oscar Gamble (OF, DH)	1977, 1985	Ted Gray (P)	1955
Chick Gandil (1B)	1910, 1917–19	Craig Grebeck (SS)	1990–95
Freddy Garcia (P)	2004–06	Danny Green (OF)	1902–05
Mike Garcia (P)	1960	Paul Gregory (P)	1932–33
Ramon Garcia (P)	1991	Clark Griffith (P)	1901–02
Jon Garland (P)	2000–06	Jason Grilli (P)	2004
Lou Garland (P)	1931	Ross Grimsley (P)	1951
Ralph Garr (OF)	1976–79	Marv Grissom (P)	1952
Hank Garrity (C)	1931	Ernest Groth (P)	1949
Ned Garvin (P)	1902	Johnny Groth (OF)	1954–55
Milt Gaston (P)	1932–34	Orval Grove (P)	1940–49
Joe Gates (2B)	1978–79	Frank Grube (C)	1931–33, 1935–36
Pete Gebrian (P)	1947	Ozzie Guillen (SS)	1985–97
Jim Geddes (P)	1972–73	Tom Gulley (OF)	1926
Johnny Gerlach (SS)	1938–39	Randy Gumpert (P)	1948–51
Al Gettel (P)	1948–49		
George Gick (P)	1937–38	**H**	
Mark Gilbert (OF)	1985	Bert Haas (1B)	1951
Brian Giles (2B)	1986	Mule Haas (OF)	1933–37
Claral Gillenwater (P)	1923	Warren Hacker (P)	1961
Bob Gillespie (P)	1947–48	Bump Hadley (P)	1932
Joe Ginsberg (C)	1960–61	Mickey Haefner (P)	1949–50
Matt Ginter (P)	2000–03	Charlie Haeger (P)	2006
Kid Gleason (2B)	1912	Bud Hafey (PR)	1935
Jerry Don Gleaton (P)	1984–85	Ed Hahn (OF)	1906–10
Ross Gload (1B)	2004–06	Hal Haid (P)	1933
Gary Glover (P)	2001–03	Jerry Hairston (OF)	1973–77, 1981–89
Bill Gogolewski (P)	1975	Sammy Hairston (C)	1951
Gordon Goldsberry (1B)	1949–51	Chet Hajduk (PH)	1941

Joe Hall (OF)	1994	Dustin Hermanson (P)	2005–06
Jack Hallett (P)	1940–41	Orlando Hernandez (P)	2005
Bill Hallman (OF)	1903	Roberto Hernandez (P)	1991–97
Dave Hamilton (P)	1975–77	Rudy Hernandez (SS)	1972
Jack Hamilton (P)	1969	Art Herring (P)	1939
Steve Hamilton (P)	1970	Ed Herrmann (C)	1967, 1969–74
Atlee Hammaker (P)	1994–95	Mike Hershberger (OF)	1961–64, 1971
Ralph Hamner (P)	1946	Joe Heving (P)	1933–34
Fred Hancock (SS)	1949	Mike Heydon (C)	1904
Ron Hansen (SS)	1963–69	Greg Hibbard (P)	1989–92
Don Hanski (1B, P)	1943–44	Kevin Hickey (P)	1981–83
John Happenny (2B)	1923	Piano Legs Hickman (OF)	1907
Pat Hardgrove (PH)	1918	Jim Hicks (OF)	1964
Jack Hardy (P)	1989	Joe Hicks (OF)	1959–60
Dave Harris (OF)	1930	Bill Higdon (OF)	1949
Spencer Harris (OF)	1925–26	Dennis Higgins (P)	1966–67
Willie Harris (2B)	2002–05	Donnie Hill (2B)	1987–88
Earl Harrist (P)	1947–48, 1953	Ken Hill (P)	2000
Jack Harshman (P)	1954–57	Marc Hill (C)	1981–86
Hub Hart (C)	1905–07	Shawn Hillegas (P)	1988–90
Fred Hartman (3B)	1901	Rich Hinton (P)	1971, 1975, 1978–79
Zaza Harvey (P)	1901	Myril Hoag (OF)	1941–42, 1944
Ziggy Hasbrook (1B)	1916–17	Oris Hockett (OF)	1945
Ron Hassey (C)	1986–87	Johnny Hodapp (OF)	1932
Fred Hatfield (3B)	1956–57	Shovel Hodge (P)	1920–22
Grady Hatton (3B)	1954	Ralph Hodgin (OF)	1943–44, 1946–48
Frankie Hayes (C)	1946	Dutch Hoffman (OF)	1929
Jackie Hayes (2B)	1932–40	Guy Hoffman (P)	1979–80, 1983
Joe Haynes (P)	1941–48	Ken Holcombe (P)	1950–52
Bill Heath (PH)	1965	Al Hollingsworth (P)	1946
Spencer Heath (P)	1920	Ducky Holmes (OF)	1903–05
Mike Heathcott (P)	1998	Harry Hooper (OF)	1921–25
Val Heim (OF)	1942	Gail Hopkins (1B)	1968–70
Woodie Held (OF)	1968–69	Marty Hopkins (3B)	1934–35
Scott Hemond (DH)	1992	Joe Horlen (P)	1961–71
Frank Hemphill (OF)	1906	Ricky Horton (P)	1988
Joe Henderson (P)	1974	Ken Hottman (OF)	1971
Ken Henderson (OF)	1973–75	Charlie Hough (P)	1991–92
Butch Henline (C)	1930–31	Joe Hovlik (P)	1911
Dutch Henry (P)	1929–30	Bruce Howard (P)	1963–67
Ray Herbert (P)	1961–64	Chris Howard (P)	1993

Fred Howard (P)	1979	Shawn Jeter (OF)	1992
Dixie Howell (P)	1955–58	D'Angelo Jimenez (2B)	2002–03
Dann Howitt (OF)	1994	Tommy John (P)	1965–71
Bobby Howry (P)	1998–2002	Pete Johns (3B)	1915
Dummy Hoy (OF)	1901	Bart Johnson (P)	1969–74, 1976–77
La Marr Hoyt (P)	1979–84	Charles Johnson (C)	2000
Hal Hudson (P)	1952–53	Connie Johnson (P)	1953, 1955–56
Frank Huelsman (OF)	1904	Dane Johnson (P)	1994
Mike Huff (OF)	1991–93	Darrell Johnson (C)	1952
Ed Hughes (C)	1902	Deron Johnson (DH)	1975
Jim Hughes (P)	1957	Don Johnson (P)	1954
Tim Hulett (3B)	1983–87	Ernie Johnson (SS)	1912, 1921–23
Johnny Humphries (P)	1941–45	Johnny Johnson (P)	1945
Bill Hunnefield (IF)	1926–30	Lamar Johnson (1B)	1974–81
Steve Huntz (2B)	1971	Lance Johnson (OF)	1988–95
Ira Hutchinson (P)	1933	Larry Johnson (C)	1978
		Mark Johnson (C)	1998–2002
I		Randy Johnson (DH)	1980
Tadahito Iguchi (2B)	2005–06	Stan Johnson (OF)	1960
Frank Isbell (IF)	1901–09	Walt Johnson (P)	1912, 1915
		Jimmy Johnston (OF)	1911
J		Jay Johnstone (OF)	1971–72
Bo Jackson (OF, DH)	1991, 1993	Stan Jok (3B)	1954–55
Charlie Jackson (PH)	1915	Smead Jolley (OF)	1930–32
Darrin Jackson (OF)	1994, 1999	Al Jones (P)	1983–85
Joe Jackson (OF)	1915–20	Barry Jones (P)	1988–90, 1993
Mike Jackson (P)	2004	Charlie Jones (OF)	1904
Ron Jackson (1B)	1954–59	Cleon Jones (OF)	1976
Elmer Jacobs (P)	1927	Davy Jones (OF)	1913
Otto Jacobs (C)	1918	Deacon Jones (1B)	1962, 1963–66
Pat Jacquez (P)	1971	Fielder Jones (OF)	1901–08
Bill James (P)	1919	Jake Jones (1B)	1941–42, 1946–47
Bob James (P)	1985	Sam Jones (P)	1932–35
Jerry Janeski (P)	1970	Stacy Jones (P)	1996
Hi Jasper (P)	1914–15	Steve Jones (P)	1967
Jesse Jefferson (P)	1975–76	Tex Jones (1B)	1911
Irv Jeffries (3B)	1930–31	Bubber Jonnard (C)	1920
Joe Jenkins (C)	1917–19	Rip Jordan (P)	1912
John Jenkins (IF)	1922	Tom Jordan (C)	1944, 1946
Bobby Jenks (P)	2005–06	Duane Josephson (C)	1965–70
Johnny Jeter (OF)	1973	Ted Jourdan (1B)	1916–18, 1920

Mike Joyce (P)	1962–63
Howie Judson (P)	1948–52

K

Jim Kaat (P)	1973–75
Frank Kalin (PH)	1943
Willie Kamm (3B)	1923–31
John Kane (SS)	1925
Matt Karchner (P)	1995–98
Ron Karkovice (C)	1986–97
Jack Katoll (P)	1901
Charlie Kavanagh (PH)	1914
Steve Kealey (P)	1971–73
Pat Keedy (3B)	1987
Bob Keegan (P)	1953–58
George Kell (3B)	1954–56
Pat Kelly (OF)	1971–76
Red Kelly (OF)	1910
Russ Kemmerer (P)	1960–62
Steve Kemp (OF)	1982
Bill Kennedy (P)	1952
Bob Kennedy (3B, OF)	1939–42, 1946–48, 1955–56, 1957
Vern Kennedy (P)	1934–37
Dick Kenworthy (3B)	1962, 1964–68
Joe Keough (PH)	1973
Gus Keriazakos (P)	1950
Jim Kern (P)	1982–83
Dickey Kerr (P)	1919–21, 1925
John Kerr (2B)	1929–31
Don Kessinger (SS)	1977–79
Brian Keyser (P)	1995–96
Joe Kiefer (P)	1920
Bruce Kimm (C)	1980
Chad Kimsey (P)	1932–33
Ellis Kinder (P)	1956–57
Eric King (P)	1989–90
Jim King (OF)	1967
Harry Kinzy (P)	1934
Don Kirkwood (P)	1977
Joe Kirrene (3B)	1950, 1954
Ron Kittle (OF)	1982–86, 1989–90, 1991

Hugo Klaerner (P)	1934
Fred Klages (P)	1966–67
Ed Klepfer (P)	1915
Ed Klieman (P)	1949
Joe Klinger (1B, C)	1930
Ted Kluszewski (1B)	1959–60
Chris Knapp (P)	1975–77
Bill Knickerbocker (2B)	1941
Bobby Knoop (2B)	1969–70
Jack Knott (P)	1938–40
Billy Koch (P)	2003–04
Don Kolloway (2B)	1940–43, 1946–49
Paul Konerko (1B)	1999–2006
Jerry Koosman (P)	1981–83
Fabian Kowalik (P)	1932
Al Kozar (2B)	1950
Ken Kravec (P)	1975–80
Mike Kreevich (OF)	1935–41
Ralph Kreitz (C)	1911
Chuck Kress (1B)	1949–50
Red Kress (1B, OF)	1932–34
Lou Kretlow (P)	1950–53
Chad Kreuter (C)	1996–98
Frank Kreutzer (P)	1962–64
Rocky Krsnich (3B)	1949, 1952–53
John Kruk (DH)	1995
Jack Kucek (P)	1974–79
Joe Kuhel (1B)	1938–43, 1946–47
Walt Kuhn (C)	1912–14
Rusty Kuntz (OF)	1979–83
Art Kusnyer (C)	1970
Jerry Kutzler (P)	1990
Bob Kuzava (P)	1949–50

L

Lerrin LaGrow (P)	1977–79
Jack Lamabe (P)	1966–67
Fred Lamline (P)	1912
Dennis Lamp (P)	1981–83
Ken Landenberger (1B)	1952
Jim Landis (OF)	1957–64
Jesse Landrum (2B)	1938

Dick Lane (OF)	1949	Kenny Lofton (OF)	2002
Frank Lange (P)	1910–13	Boone Logan (P)	2006
Paul LaPalme (P)	1956–57	Ron Lolich (OF)	1971
Dave LaPoint (P)	1987–88	Sherm Lollar (C)	1952–63
Jack Lapp (C)	1916	Tim Lollar (P)	1985
Don Larsen (P)	1961	Bill Long (P)	1985, 1987–90
Frank Lary (P)	1965	Jeoff Long (1B, OF)	1964
Bill Lathrop (P)	1913–14	Jimmie Long (C)	1922
Barry Latman (P)	1957–59	Dean Look (OF)	1961
Mike LaValliere (C)	1993–95	Ed Lopat (P)	1944–47
Rudy Law (OF)	1982–85	Pedro Lopez (2B, SS)	2005
Vance Law (3B)	1982–84	Harry Lord (3B)	1910–14
Bob Lawrence (P)	1924	Andrew Lorraine (P)	1995
Danny Lazar (P)	1968–69	Mem Lovett (PH)	1933
Terry Leach (P)	1992–93	Jay Loviglio (2B)	1981–82
Carlos Lee (OF)	1999–2004	Grover Lowdermilk (P)	1919–20
Thornton Lee (P)	1937	Sean Lowe (P)	1999–2001
George Lees (C)	1921	Turk Lown (P)	1958–62
Ron LeFlore (OF)	1981–82	David Lundquist (P)	1999
Paul Lehner (OF)	1951	Tony Lupien (1B)	1948
Nemo Leibold (OF)	1915–20	Greg Luzinski (DH)	1981–84
Elmer Leifer (3B, OF)	1921	Sparky Lyle (P)	1982
Dummy Leitner (P)	1902	Byrd Lynn (C)	1916–20
Chet Lemon (OF)	1975–81	Barry Lyons (C)	1995
Jim Lemon (1B)	1963	Steve Lyons (IF, OF)	1986–90
Dave Lemonds (P)	1972	Ted Lyons (P)	1923–42, 1946
Don Lenhardt (OF)	1951	Jim Lyttle (OF)	1972
Eddie Leon (SS)	1973–74		
Rudy Leopold (P)	1928	**M**	
Ted Lepcio (3B)	1961	Mike MacDougal (P)	2006
Dixie Leverett (P)	1922–24, 1926	Robert Machado (C)	1996–98
Alan Levine (P)	1996	Frank Mack (P)	1922–23, 1925
Darren Lewis (OF)	1996–97	Rob Mackowiak (OF)	2006
Jeff Liefer (1B, OF)	1999–2002	Ed Madjeski (C)	1934
Bill Lindsey (C)	1987	Jim Magnuson (P)	1970–71
Doug Lindsey (C)	1993	George Magoon (2B)	1903
Chuck Lindstrom (C)	1958	Joe Magrane (P)	1996
Bryan Little (2B)	1985–86	Bob Mahoney (P)	1951
Dick Littlefield (P)	1951	Hank Majeski (3B)	1950–51
Esteban Loaiza (P)	2003–04	Jule Mallonee (OF)	1925
Bob Locker (P)	1965–69	Eddie Malone (C)	1949–50
Dario Lodigiani (3B)	1941–42, 1946	Gordon Maltzberger (P)	1943–44, 1946–47

Carl Manda (2B)	1914	Tommy McCraw (1B)	1963–70
Leo Mangum (P)	1924–25	Rodney McCray (OF)	1990–91
Johnny Mann (3B)	1928	Harry McCurdy (C)	1926–28
Fred Manrique (2B)	1987–89	Jim McDonald (P)	1956–58
Moxie Manuel (P)	1908	Jack McDowell (P)	1987–88, 1990–94
Ravelo Manzanillo (P)	1988	Chuck McElroy (P)	1997
Johnny Marcum (P)	1939	Ed McFarland (C)	1902–07
Dick Marlowe (P)	1956	Herm McFarland (OF)	1901–02
Isidro Marquez (P)	1995	Ed McGhee (OF)	1950, 1954–55
Fred Marsh (3B)	1953–54	Lynn McGlothen (P)	1981
Willard Marshall (OF)	1954–55	Jim McGlothlin (P)	1973
Damaso Marte (P)	2002–05	Tom McGuire (P)	1919
J. C. Martin (C)	1959–67	Stover McIlwain (P)	1957–58
Joe Martin (PR)	1938	Matty McIntyre (OF)	1911–12
Morrie Martin (P)	1954–56	Hal McKain (P)	1929–32
Norberto Martin (2B, SS)	1993–97	Joel McKeon (P)	1986–87
Carlos Martinez (3B, 1B)	1988–90	Rich McKinney (IF, OF)	1970–71
Dave Martinez (OF)	1995–97	Polly McLarry (PH)	1912
Silvio Martinez (P)	1977	Cal McLish (P)	1961
Randy Martz (P)	1983	Sam McMackin (P)	1902
Phil Masi (C)	1950–52	Don McMahon (P)	1967
John Matias (OF)	1970	Fred McMullin (3B)	1916–20
Wally Mattick (OF)	1912–13	Eric McNair (IF)	1939–40
Mark Mauldin (3B)	1934	Jerry McNertney (C)	1964, 1966–68
Charlie Maxwell (OF)	1962–64	Doug McWeeny (P)	1921–22, 1924
Carlos May (1B, OF)	1968–76	Sam Mele (OF)	1952–53
Milt May (C)	1979	Paul Meloan (OF)	1910–11
Lee Maye (OF)	1970–71	Bill Melton (3B)	1968–75
Erskine Mayer (P)	1919	Bob Melvin (C)	1994
Wally Mayer (C)	1911–12, 1914–15	Lloyd Merriman (PH)	1955
Jack McAleese (P)	1901	Sam Mertes (2B, OF)	1901–02
Jim McAnany (OF)	1958–60	Matt Merullo (C)	1989, 1991–93
Pryor McBee (P)	1926	Bobby Messenger (OF)	1909–11
Ken McBride (P)	1959–60	Catfish Metkovich (OF)	1949
Dick McCabe (P)	1922	William Metzig (2B)	1944
Brian McCall (OF)	1962–63	Alex Metzler (OF)	1927–30
Brandon McCarthy (P)	2005–06	Billy Meyer (C)	1913
Tom McCarthy (P)	1988–89	George Meyer (2B)	1938
Kirk McCaskill (P)	1992–96	Cass Michaels (IF)	1943–50, 1954
Harvey McClellan (SS)	1919–24	John Michaelson (P)	1921
Amby McConnell (2B)	1910–11	Aaron Miles (2B)	2003
Mike McCormick (OF)	1950	Bob Miller (P)	1970

Frank Miller (P)	1913
Jake Miller (P)	1933
Minnie Minoso (OF)	1951–57, 1960–61,
	1964, 1976, 1980
Willy Miranda (SS)	1952
Roy Mitchell (P)	1918
George Mogridge (P)	1911–12
Bob Molinaro (OF)	1977–78, 1980–81
Rich Moloney (P)	1970
Larry Monroe (P)	1976
Aurelio Monteagudo (P)	1967
Agustin Montero (P)	2006
Barry Moore (P)	1970
Jim Moore (P)	1930–32
Jimmy Moore (OF)	1930
Junior Moore (3B, OF)	1978–80
Randy Moore (OF)	1927–28
Ray Moore (P)	1958–60
Rich Morales (IF)	1967–73
Bill Moran (P)	1974
Ray Morehart (2B, SS)	1924, 1926
George Moriarty (1B, 3B)	1916
Russ Morman (1B)	1986, 1988–89
Bugs Morris (P)	1921
Jim Morrison (2B, 3B)	1979–82
Jo-Jo Morrissey (IF)	1936
Gerry Moses (1B)	1975
Wally Moses (OF)	1942–46
Les Moss (C)	1955–58
Don Mossi (P)	1964
Johnny Mostil (OF)	1918, 1921–29
Glen Moulder (P)	1948
Lyle Mouton (OF)	1995–97
Bill Mueller (OF)	1942–45
Don Mueller (OF)	1958–59
Greg Mulleavy (SS)	1930, 1932
Charlie Mullen (1B)	1910–11
Eddie Mulligan (3B)	1921–22
Fran Mullins (3B)	1980
Dominic Mulrenan (P)	1921
Arnie Munoz (P)	2004
Jose Munoz (2B)	1996

Steve Mura (P)	1983
Danny Murphy (P)	1969–70
Eddie Murphy (OF)	1915–21
George Murray (P)	1933
Tony Muser (1B)	1971–75
Aaron Myette (P)	1999–2000

N

Bill Nagel (1B)	1945
Bill Nahorodny (C)	1977–79
Frank Naleway (SS)	1924
Cotton Nash (1B)	1967
Jaime Navarro (P)	1997–99
Bernie Neis (OF)	1927
Andy Nelson (P)	1908
Gene Nelson (P)	1984–86
Jeff Nelson (P)	2006
Rocky Nelson (PH)	1951
Roger Nelson (P)	1967
Jack Ness (1B)	1916
Dan Neumeier (P)	1972
Warren Newson (OF)	1991–95
Gus Niarhos (C)	1950–51
Don Nicholas (OF)	1952, 1954
Reid Nichols (OF)	1985–86
Dave Nicholson (OF)	1963–65
Scott Nielsen (P)	1987
Bob Nieman (OF)	1955–56
Randy Niemann (P)	1984
Tim Nordbrook (SS)	1977
Wayne Nordhagen (OF)	1976–81
Bill Norman (OF)	1931–32
Ron Northey (PH)	1955–57
Greg Norton (1B, 3B)	1996–2000
Win Noyes (P)	1919
Chris Nyman (1B)	1982–83
Jerry Nyman (P)	1968–69
Nyls Nyman (OF)	1974–77

O

Buck O'Brien (P)	1913
Charlie O'Brien (C)	1998

Syd O'Brien (3B)	1970	Roy Patterson (P)	1901–07
Tom O'Malley (3B)	1984	Josh Paul (C)	1999–2003
Bill O'Neill (OF)	1906	Don Pavletich (C)	1969
Emmett O'Neill (P)	1946	John Pawlowski (P)	1987–88
Denny O'Toole (P)	1969–73	Fred Payne (C)	1909–11
Jim O'Toole (P)	1967	George Payne (P)	1920
Blue Moon Odom (P)	1976	Ike Pearson (P)	1948
Miguel Olivo (C)	2002–04	Roger Peckinpaugh (SS)	1927
Fred Olmstead (P)	1908–11	Jesus Pena (P)	1999
Magglio Ordonez (OF)	1997–2004	Tony Pena (C)	1997
Joe Orengo (3B)	1945	Elmer Pence (OF)	1922
Jorge Orta (2B)	1972–79	Russ Pence (P)	1921
Jose Ortiz (OF)	1969–70	Jack Perconte (2B)	1986
Danny Osborn (P)	1975	Melido Perez (P)	1988–91
Dan Osinski (P)	1969	Timo Perez (OF)	2004–05
Claude Osteen (P)	1975	John Perkovich (P)	1950
Red Ostergard (PH)	1921	Len Perme (P)	1942, 1946
Johnny Ostrowski (OF)	1949–50	Herbert Perry (3B)	2000–01
Antonio Osuna (P)	2001–02	Stan Perzanowski (P)	1971, 1974
Jim Otten (P)	1974–76	Gary Peters (P)	1959
Frank Owen (P)	1903–09	Rube Peters (P)	1912
Marv Owen (3B)	1938–39	Adam Peterson (P)	1987–90
Frank Owens (C)	1909	Buddy Peterson (SS)	1955
Jerry Owens (OF)	2006	Ray Phelps (P)	1935–36
Pablo Ozuna (IF, OF)	2005–06	Dave Philley (OF)	1941, 1946–51, 1956–57
		Bubba Phillips (3B)	1956–59
P		Taylor Phillips (P)	1963
Tom Paciorek (1B, OF)	1982–85	Tony Phillips (OF)	1996–97
Del Paddock (PH)	1912	Wiley Piatt (P)	1901–02
Donn Pall (P)	1988–93	Billy Pierce (P)	1949–61
Jose Paniagua (P)	2003	Marino Pieretti (P)	1948–49
Al Papai (P)	1955	A. J. Pierzynski (C)	2005–06
Frank Papish (P)	1945–48	Tony Piet (2B, 3B)	1935–37
Freddy Parent (SS)	1908–11	Al Pilarcik (OF)	1961
Kelly Paris (1B)	1988	Babe Pinelli (3B)	1918
Jim Parque (P)	1998–2002	Skip Pitlock (P)	1974–75
Casey Parsons (OF)	1983–84	Juan Pizarro (P)	1961–66
Johnny Pasek (C)	1934	Whitey Platt (OF)	1946
Dan Pasqua (OF)	1988–94	Scott Podsednik (OF)	2005–06
Ham Patterson (1B)	1909	Cliff Politte (P)	2004–06
Ken Patterson (P)	1988–91	Howie Pollet (P)	1956
Reggie Patterson (P)	1981	John Pomorski (P)	1934

Irv Porter (OF)	1914
Mike Porzio (P)	2002–03
Bob Poser (P)	1932
Bob Powell (PR)	1955, 1957
Frank Pratt (PH)	1921
Bob Priddy (P)	1968–69
Red Proctor (P)	1923
Mike Proly (P)	1978–80
Ron Pruitt (OF)	1980
Greg Pryor (IF)	1978–81
Bill Pulsipher (P)	2001
Pid Purdy (OF)	1926
Billy Purtell (3B)	1908–10

Q

Jim Qualls (OF)	1972
Tom Qualters (P)	1958
Lee Quillen (3B)	1906–07
Finners Quinlan (OF)	1915
Jack Quinn (P)	1918
Jamie Quirk (3B)	1984

R

Rip Radcliff (OF)	1934–39
Don Rader (OF, 3B)	1913
Scott Radinsky (P)	1990–93, 1995
Pat Ragan (P)	1919
Tim Raines (OF)	1991–95
Julio Ramirez (OF)	2001
Jim Randall (1B, OF)	1988
Earl Rapp (OF)	1949
Fred Rath (P)	1968–69
Morrie Rath (2B)	1912–13
Jon Rauch (P)	2002, 2004
Claude Raymond (P)	1959
Buck Redfern (IF)	1928–29
Gary Redus (OF)	1987–88
Ron Reed (P)	1984
Phil Regan (P)	1972
Rick Reichardt (OF)	1971–73
Barney Reilly (2B)	1909
Steve Renko (P)	1977

Tony Rensa (C)	1937–39
Jerry Reuss (P)	1988–89
Carl Reynolds (OF)	1927–31
Danny Reynolds (SS, 2B)	1945
Bobby Rhawn (3B)	1949
Hal Rhyne (IF)	1933
Dennis Ribant (P)	1968
Lee Richard (IF)	1971–72, 1974–75
Marv Rickert (OF)	1950
Johnny Riddle (C)	1930
Dave Righetti (P)	1995
Johnny Rigney (P)	1937–42, 1946–47
Armando Rios (OF)	2003
Swede Risberg (SS)	1917–20
David Riske (P)	2006
Todd Ritchie (P)	2002
Jim Rivera (OF)	1952–61
Tink Riviere (P)	1925
Todd Rizzo (P)	1998–99
Bert Roberge (P)	1984
Charlie Robertson (P)	1919, 1922–25
Mike Robertson (1B, DH)	1996
Billy Jo Robidoux (1B)	1989
Aaron Robinson (C)	1948
Dewey Robinson (P)	1979–81
Eddie Robinson (1B)	1950–52
Floyd Robinson (OF)	1960–66
Les Rock (1B)	1936
Aurelio Rodriguez (3B)	1982–83
Hector Rodriguez (3B)	1952
Liu Rodriguez (IF)	1999
Saul Rogovin (P)	1951–53
George Rohe (3B)	1905–07
Johnny Romano (C)	1958–59, 1965–66
Vicente Romo (P)	1971–72
Gilberto Rondon (P)	1979
Phil Roof (C)	1976
Bob Roselli (C)	1961–62
Lou Rosenberg (2B)	1923
Steve Rosenberg (P)	1988–90
Larry Rosenthal (OF)	1936–41
Buck Ross (P)	1941–45

Marv Rotblatt (P)	1948, 1950–51
Braggo Roth (OF)	1914–15
Frank Roth (C)	1906
Jack Rothrock (OF)	1932
Gene Rounsaville (P)	1970
Edd Roush (OF)	1913
Aaron Rowand (OF)	2001–05
Jerry Royster (3B)	1987
Don Rudolph (P)	1957–59
Muddy Ruel (C)	1934
Scott Ruffcorn (P)	1993–96
Red Ruffing (P)	1947
Bob Rush (P)	1960
John Russell (P)	1921–22
Reb Russell (P)	1913–19
Mark Ryal (OF)	1985
Blondy Ryan (3B)	1930
Connie Ryan (3B)	1953

S

Chris Sabo (DH)	1995
Bob Sadowski (3B, 2B)	1962
Olmedo Saenz (3B)	1994
Mark Salas (C)	1988
Luis Salazar (OF)	1985–86
Bill Salkeld (C)	1950
Jack Salveson (P)	1935
David Sanders (P)	2003, 2005
Scott Sanderson (P)	1994
Ron Santo (DH, IF)	1974
Nelson Santovenia (C)	1992
Rich Sauveur (P)	1996
Carl Sawatski (C)	1954
Steve Sax (2B, OF)	1992–93
Jerry Scala (OF)	1948–50
Randy Scarbery (P)	1979–80
Ray Scarborough (P)	1950
Jeff Schaefer (IF)	1989
Jimmie Schaffer (C)	1965
Ray Schalk (C)	1912–28
Roy Schalk (2B)	1944–45
Biff Schaller (OF)	1913

Norm Schlueter (C)	1938–39
Dave Schmidt (P)	1986
Scott Schoeneweis (P)	2003–04
Ossee Schreckengost (C)	1908
Hank Schreiber (OF)	1914
Ron Schueler (P)	1978–79
Webb Schultz (P)	1924
Ferdie Schupp (P)	1922
Jeff Schwarz (P)	1993–94
Jim Scoggins (P)	1913
Herb Score (P)	1960–62
Everett Scott (SS)	1926
Jim Scott (P)	1909–17
Ray Searage (P)	1986–87
Tom Seaver (P)	1984–86
Don Secrist (P)	1969–70
Bob Seeds (OF)	1932
Pat Seerey (OF)	1948–49
Jose Segura (P)	1988–89
Ricky Seilheimer (C)	1980
Carey Selph (3B, 2B)	1932
Luke Sewell (C)	1935–38
Bill Sharp (OF)	1973–75
Al Shaw (C)	1908
Bob Shaw (P)	1958–61
Jeff Shaw (P)	1995
Merv Shea (C)	1934–37
Bud Sheely (C)	1951–53
Earl Sheely (1B)	1921–27
Frank Shellenback (P)	1918–19
Joe Shipley (P)	1963
Art Shires (1B)	1928–30
Ray Shook (PR)	1916
Bill Shores (P)	1936
Dave Short (OF)	1940–41
Clyde Shoun (P)	1949
Frank Shugart (SS)	1901
Ruben Sierra (OF)	1998
Roy Sievers (1B)	1960–61
Frank Sigafoos (2B)	1929
Ken Silvestri (C)	1939–40
Al Sima (P)	1954

Bill Simas (P)	1995–2000	Dan Spillner (P)	1984–85
Al Simmons (OF)	1933–35	Mike Squires (1B)	1975, 1977–85
Brian Simmons (OF)	1998–99	Marv Staehle (2B)	1964–67
Mel Simons (OF)	1931–32	Gerry Staley (P)	1956–61
Harry Simpson (OF)	1959	Lee Stange (P)	1970
Chris Singleton (OF)	1999–2001	Joe Stanka (P)	1959
Mike Sirotka (P)	1995–2000	Mike Stanton (P)	1985
Tommie Sisk (P)	1970	Matt Stark (DH)	1990
Jim Siwy (P)	1982, 1984	Milt Steengrafe (P)	1924, 1926
Bud Sketchley (OF)	1942	Dave Stegman (OF)	1983–84
Joel Skinner (C)	1983–86	Bill Stein (2B, 3B)	1974–76
Lou Skizas (OF)	1959	Hank Steinbacher (OF)	1937–39
John Skopec (P)	1901	Gene Stephens (OF)	1963–64
Bill Skowron (1B)	1964–67	Vern Stephens (3B)	1953, 1955
Jack Slattery (C)	1903	Joe Stephenson (C)	1947
Don Slaught (C)	1996	Bud Stewart (OF)	1951–54
Roy Smalley (3B)	1984	Chris Stewart (C)	2006
Joe Smaza (OF)	1946	Frank Stewart (P)	1927
Al Smith (OF, 3B)	1958–62	Jimmy Stewart (OF, IF)	1967
Art Smith (P)	1932	Josh Stewart (P)	2003–04
Bob Smith (P)	1913	Dave Stieb (P)	1993
Charley Smith (3B)	1962–64	Royle Stillman (OF)	1977
Eddie Smith (P)	1939–43, 1946–47	Lee Stine (P)	1934–35
Ernie Smith (SS)	1930	Chuck Stobbs (P)	1952
Frank Smith (P)	1904–10	Tim Stoddard (P)	1975
Harry Smith (P)	1912	Dean Stone (P)	1962
Pop Boy Smith (P)	1913	Steve Stone (P)	1973, 1977–78
Roxy Snipes (PH)	1923	John Stoneham (OF)	1933
Chris Snopek (IF)	1995–98	Dick Strahs (P)	1954
Cory Snyder (OF, 1B)	1991	Sammy Strang (3B)	1902
John Snyder (P)	1998–99	Monty Stratton (P)	1934–38
Russ Snyder (OF)	1968	Elmer Stricklett (P)	1904
Eric Soderholm (3B)	1977–79	Jake Striker (P)	1960
Eddie Solomon (P)	1982	Ed Stroud (OF)	1966–67, 1971
Moose Solters (OF)	1940–41, 1943	Amos Strunk (OF)	1920–24
Sammy Sosa (OF)	1989–91	George Stumpf (OF)	1936
Steve Souchock (OF, 1B)	1949	Tanyon Sturtze (P)	1999–2000
Floyd Speer (P)	1943–44	Joe Sugden (C)	1901
Bob Spence (1B)	1969–71	Billy Sullivan (C)	1901–12, 1914
Jim Spencer (1B)	1976–77	Billy Sullivan (3B, 1B)	1931–33
Tom Spencer (OF)	1978	John Sullivan (P)	1919
Ed Spiezio (3B)	1972	Scott Sullivan (P)	2003

Max Surkont (P)	1949	Earl Torgeson (1B)	1957–61
Rube Suter (P)	1909	Pablo Torrealba (P)	1978–79
Leo Sutherland (OF)	1980–81	Rusty Torres (OF)	1978–79
Dale Sveum (SS)	1992	Clay Touchstone (P)	1945
Evar Swanson (OF)	1932–34	Babe Towne (C)	1906
Karl Swanson (2B)	1928–29	Sean Tracey (P)	2006
Ryan Sweeney (OF)	2006	Chris Tremie (C)	1995
Augie Swentor (C)	1922	Mike Tresh (C)	1938–48
Bill Swift (P)	1943	Hal Trosky (1B)	1944, 1946
		Hal Trosky (P)	1958
T		Steve Trout (P)	1978–82
Doug Taitt (OF)	1929	Virgil Trucks (P)	1953–55
Shingo Takatsu (P)	2004–05	Thurman Tucker (OF)	1942–44, 1946–47
Fred Talbot (P)	1963–64	Jerry Turner (OF)	1981
Leo Tankersley (C)	1925	Tom Turner (C)	1940–44
Lee Tannehill (3B, SS)	1903–12	Cy Twombly (P)	1921
Bruce Tanner (P)	1985		
Kevin Tapani (P)	1996	**U**	
Danny Tartabull (OF)	1996	Frenchy Uhalt (OF)	1934
Bennie Tate (C)	1930–32	Bob Uhl (P)	1938
Ken Tatum (P)	1974	Charlie Uhlir (OF)	1934
Fred Tauby (OF)	1935	Cecil Upshaw (P)	1975
Leo Taylor (PR)	1923	Juan Uribe (SS)	2004–06
Wiley Taylor (P)	1912		
Zeb Terry (SS)	1916–17	**V**	
Bobby Thigpen (P)	1986–93	Mario Valdez (1B)	1997
Frank Thomas (1B, DH)	1990–2005	Wilson Valdez (SS, 2B)	2004
Larry Thomas (P)	1995–97	Jose Valentin (SS, 3B)	2000–04
Leo Thomas (3B)	1952	Vito Valentinetti (P)	1954
Tommy Thomas (P)	1926–32	Joe Vance (P)	1935
Jim Thome (DH)	2006	Pete Varney (C)	1973–76
Lee Thompson (P)	1921	Javier Vazquez (P)	2006
Tommy Thompson (1B)	1938–39	Pat Veltman (SS)	1926
Matt Thornton (P)	2006	Robin Ventura (3B)	1989–98
Sloppy Thurston (P)	1923–26	John Verhoeven (P)	1977
Dick Tidrow (P)	1983	Ken Vining (P)	2001
Verle Tiefenthaler (P)	1962	Rube Vinson (OF)	1906
Les Tietje (P)	1933–36	Luis Vizcaino (P)	2005
Ron Tingley (C)	1994	Fritz Von Kolnitz (3B)	1916
Joe Tipton (C)	1949	Bill Voss (OF)	1965
Wayne Tolleson (3B)	1986	Pete Vuckovich (P)	1975–76

W

Jake Wade (P)	1942–44
Leon Wagner (OF)	1968
Don Wakamatsu (C)	1991
Dixie Walker (OF)	1936–37
Gee Walker (OF)	1938–39
Greg Walker (1B)	1982–90
Kevin Walker (P)	2005
Jack Wallaesa (SS, OF)	1947–48
Ed Walsh (P)	1904–16
Ed Walsh (P)	1928–30, 1932
Steve Wapnick (P)	1991
Aaron Ward (2B)	1927
Bryan Ward (P)	1998–99
Pete Ward (3B, OF)	1963–69
Claudell Washington (OF)	1978–80
George Washington (OF)	1935–36
Johnny Watwood (OF, 1B)	1929–32
Bob Way (2B)	1927
Art Weaver (C)	1908
Buck Weaver (SS, 3B)	1912–20
Floyd Weaver (P)	1970
Earl Webb (OF)	1933
Skeeter Webb (SS, 2B)	1940–44
Biggs Wehde (P)	1930–31
Dave Wehrmeister (P)	1985
Ralph Weigel (C)	1948
Bob Weiland (P)	1928–31
Ed Weiland (P)	1940, 1942
Al Weis (2B, SS)	1962–67
Mike Welday (OF)	1907, 1909
David Wells (P)	2001
Kip Wells (P)	1999–2001
Leo Wells (3B, SS)	1942, 1946
Sammy West (OF)	1942
Don Wheeler (C)	1949
Doc White (P, OF)	1903–13
Ed White (OF)	1955
Rick White (P)	2003
John Whitehead (P)	1935–39
Frank Whitman (SS)	1946, 1948

Chris Widger (C)	2005–06
Al Widmar (P)	1952
Jack Wieneke (P)	1921
Bill Wight (P)	1948–50
Randy Wiles (P)	1977
Hoyt Wilhelm (P)	1963–68
Roy Wilkinson (P)	1919–22
Jerry Willard (C)	1990
Eddie Williams (3B)	1989
Kenny Williams (OF)	1986–88
Lefty Williams (P)	1916–20
Walt Williams (OF)	1967–72
Al Williamson (P)	1928
Hugh Willingham (2B)	1930
Carl Willis (P)	1988
Jim Willoughby (P)	1978
Ted Wills (P)	1965
Kid Willson (OF)	1918, 1927
Bill Wilson (OF)	1950, 1953–54
Craig Wilson (IF)	1998–2000
Jim Wilson (P)	1956–58
Red Wilson (C)	1951–54
Roy Wilson (P)	1928–28
Ted Wilson (1B)	1952
Jim Winn (P)	1987
Kettle Wirts (C)	1924
Archie Wise (P)	1932
Polly Wolfe (OF)	1912, 1914
Mellie Wolfgang (P)	1914–18
Wilbur Wood (P)	1967–78
Mike Woodard (2B)	1988
Frank Woodward (P)	1923
Rich Wortham (P)	1978–80
Al Worthington (P)	1960
Cy Wright (SS)	1916
Dan Wright (P)	2001–04
Glenn Wright (2B)	1935
Taffy Wright (OF)	1940–42, 1946–48
Tom Wright (OF)	1952–53
Rick Wrona (C)	1993
Kelly Wunsch (P)	2000–04

Whit Wyatt (P)	1933–36
Early Wynn (P)	1958–62
Billy Wynne (P)	1968–70

Y

Hugh Yancy (3B, 2B)	1972, 1974, 1976
George Yankowski (C)	1949
Yam Yaryan (C)	1921–22
Rudy York (1B)	1947
Irv Young (P)	1910–11

Z

Dom Zanni (P)	1962–63
Al Zarilla (OF)	1951–52
Rollie Zeider (IF)	1910–13
Gus Zernial (OF)	1949–51
Richie Zisk (OF)	1977
Bob Zupcic (OF)	1994
Dutch Zwilling (OF)	1910